Bill Harvey

The Gambit Files

Tactical Themes to Sharpen Your Play

MONGOOSE
Press

BOSTON

Publisher: Mongoose Press
1005 Boylston Street, Suite 324
Newton Highlands, MA 02461
info@mongoosepress.com
www.MongoosePress.com
ISBN: 978-1-9362771-1-7
Library of Congress Control Number: 2010936943
Distributed to the trade by National Book Network
custserv@nbnbooks.com, 800-462-6420
For all other sales inquiries please contact the Publisher.

Layout: Semko Semkov
Editor: Jorge Amador
Cover Design: Creative Center – Bulgaria
First English edition
0 9 8 7 6 5 4 3 2 1
Printed in China

Contents

Introduction

Long before I learned how to read chess notation, I remember marveling over the final position in the famous "Shower of Gold" game, Levitsky-Marshall, Breslau 1912. Notation can make a game permanent, but it is the winning combination that captures a young explorer's attention. In any opening, characteristic strategies yield typical tactics. A good grounding in the combinations that we are likely to face in the opening we wish to master gives us a clearer understanding and appreciation of that opening.

Gambits are a remedy for chessplayers who have become complacent. As King Solomon would say, "Don't set your heart on your wealth, but never say, 'I have enough.'" Studying gambits makes us better people: There's greed and fear, along with braggadocio and uncertainty – and to some extent, there's an equal measure of each. This is exactly what gets in the way of formalized gambit study. Memorizing lines often leads to cold, unemotional middlegames. This is not really what the student seeks.

For this book I have reviewed thousands of chess games for interesting combinations, relying on the engines *Rybka* 3 and *Fritz* 6 to verify that the combinations here are sound and unique. These positions should give the reader a good idea of the kind of power that must be harnessed, or faced, in a gambit. Following the review of the themes and strategies for each gambit, I have provided a collection of puzzles taken from miniatures to help to improve the reader's understanding of the variation. The solutions are given at the end of the book, with their starting diagrams for convenience.

Bill Harvey
Alexandria, Virginia
May 2010

Chapter 1

The Lisitsin Gambit (A04)

This opening is named for the Soviet IM Georgy Lisitsin, though its early development also depended on the work of the Yugoslav grandmaster Vasja Pirc. The gambit is also known as the Pirc-Lisitsin.

1. ♘f3 f5 2. e4 fxe4 3. ♘g5:

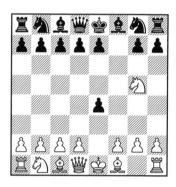

Black normally returns the pawn, in the variations 3...♘f6 4. d3 e3 5. ♗xe3 e5; 3...d5 4. d3 ♕d6; and 3...e5 4. d3 e3 5. ♗xe3. If Black wishes to keep the pawn, the main line is 3...♘f6 4. d3 d5 5. dxe4 h6 6. ♘f3 dxe4 7. ♕xd8+ ♔xd8 8. ♘e5, leading to the following position:

(See next diagram)

Black has few assets other than the extra pawn, and his position is riddled with weaknesses. Still, the opening creates some unique combinations.

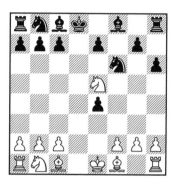

In the example below, White is a strong master and Black is an expert, but White sacrifices a bishop and finishes the game in 10 moves.

**Sergey Stoljarov – Vasily Rusnak
Kolontaevo 1998**

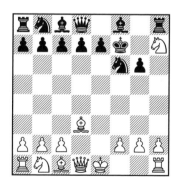

7. ♘g5+ ♔g7 (7...♔g8 8. ♗xg6 ♖h4 9. ♘e6) 8. ♗xg6 ♔xg6 9. ♕d3+ ♔g7 10. ♘e6+ 1-0

White sacrifices the g5-knight and comes very close to queening a pawn in the first ten moves.

Alexey Druzhinin – Alexander Babanov, Moscow 2007

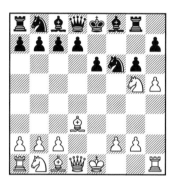

8. ♘xh7 ♘xh7 (8...gxh5 9. ♗g5 ♗b4+ 10. c3 ♖xg5 11. ♘xg5 ♗c5 12. ♖xh5) 9. ♗xg6+ ♖xg6 10. hxg6 ♘f6 11. ♖h8 ♔e7 12. g7 ♗xg7 13. ♖xd8 ♔xd8 14. ♗g5 ♔e7 15. ♕h5 ♔f8 16. ♕g6 ♘g8 17. ♘c3 d6 18. 0-0-0 ♘c6 19. ♘b5 ♘e5 20. ♕h5 ♘f7 21. ♘xc7 1-0

Rybka rates White as having a piece's worth of advantage here. White's pieces are more active, and a sacrifice is affordable.

Michael Geveke – Roland Storm Germany 1983

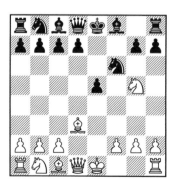

6. ♗xh7 ♘xh7 (6...♖xh7 7. ♘xh7) 7. ♕h5+ ♔e7 8. ♘xh7 ♔d6 9. ♕g6+ ♔c5 10. ♗e3+ ♔b5 11. a4+ ♔a5 12. ♗d2+ ♔b4 13. c3 ♗d6 14. b4+ ♔b6 15. ♗e3+ c5 16. ♗xc5+ ♔a6 17. ♕d3+ 1-0

The following game highlights the weaknesses in Black's position. White picks up at least the exchange.

Janez Barle – Richard Tozer London 1993

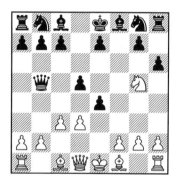

8. ♕h5+ ♔d7 9. ♕g4+ ♔c6 (9...♔d8 10. ♘f7+ ♔e8 11. ♕g6) 10. ♕xc8 ♘d7 11. ♕xa8 hxg5 12. dxe4 ♕b6 13. exd5+ ♔xd5 14. ♗e2 e5 15. ♗e3 1-0

Black has weaknesses on the queenside too.

Šarūnas Šulskis – Przemysław Koc Koszalin 1998

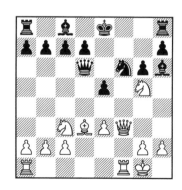

14. ♘b5 ♛b6 15. ♘xc7+ ♛xc7 16.
♛xf6 ♖f8 17. ♘f7 ♝xe3+ 18. ♚h1 ♝c5
19. ♖ae1 ♝e7 20. ♖xe5 ♛xe5 1-0

Although White has two pieces
hanging, he can save them easily. The
knight on h7, far from being out of
play, is actually quite effective.

Franz Haselbeck – G. Spiessberger
Niederbayern 1999

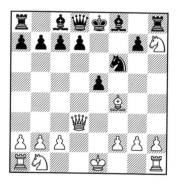

9. ♛g6+ ♚e7 10. ♝g5 ♚e6 11. ♝xf6
gxf6 12. ♘g5+ ♚d5 13. ♘c3+ ♚c6 14.
♛e4+ 1-0 (14...d5 15. ♛a4+ ♚d6 16.
♘f7+)

Puzzles

Taking time to understand the na-
ture of an opening can be a fruitful
exercise. Solve these positions from
Lisitsin Gambit encounters.
(Solutions on p. 108.)

White to move:

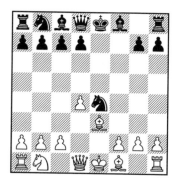

White to move:

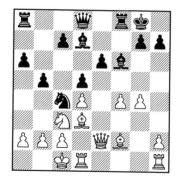

White to move:

White to move:

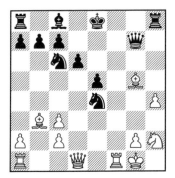

White to move:

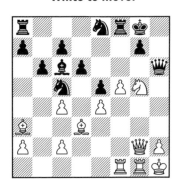

White to move:

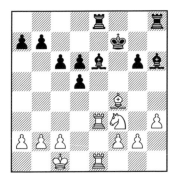

White to move:

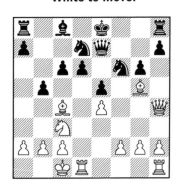

White to move:

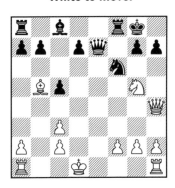

White to move:

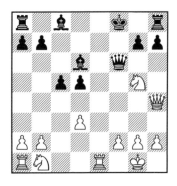

White to move:

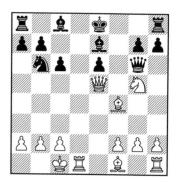

Black to move:

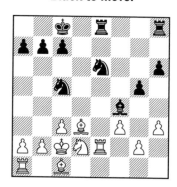

White to move:

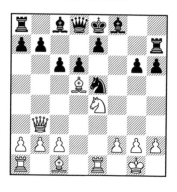

Black to move:

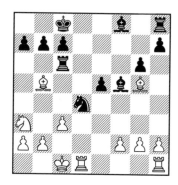

White to move:

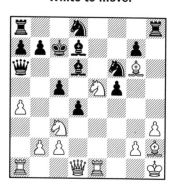

Black to move:

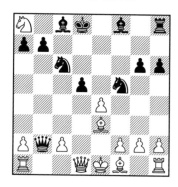

Black to move:

Black to move:

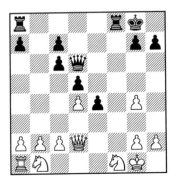

Chapter 2

///

Scandinavian Defense – Portuguese Gambit (B01)

This chapter covers the opening 1. e4 d5 2. exd5 ♘f6 3. d4 ♗g4, known as the Jadoul Variation of the Scandinavian Defense. Though often called the Portuguese Gambit, for the most part it is not a real gambit.

1. e4 d5 2. exd5 ♘f6 3. d4 ♗g4 4. f3 ♗f5 5. ♗b5+ ♘bd7 6. c4:

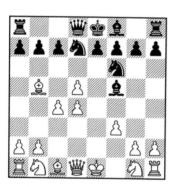

This is the most likely position White will achieve if he strives to keep the extra pawn. Black hopes for an open e-file and usually trades his e-pawn for White's d-pawn early on; then he either chases off the b5-bishop or trades it for the d7-knight and bears down the e-file with the rooks.

Every other major variation allows Black to recover his pawn – usually with the queen. Here are the most popular positions.

1. e4 d5 2. exd5 ♘f6 3. d4 ♗g4 4. ♗e2 ♗xe2 5. ♕xe2 ♕xd5 6. ♘f3 e6 7. 0-0 ♘c6:

and 1. e4 d5 2. exd5 ♘f6 3. d4 ♗g4 4. ♘f3 ♕xd5 5. ♗e2 ♘c6 6. c4 ♕h5:

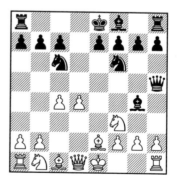

These are wide open positions, and White can develop at the expense of the misplaced queen.

Let us examine this in two sections: the Portuguese Gambit proper, and the non-gambit lines. First, the Portuguese.

Black castles into the makings of a pawn storm – and yet GM Volokitin easily rolls up the pawns.

Jan Werle – Andrei Volokitin
Groningen 1999

15...♗d3 16. ♗h6 (16. b3 ♗a3#) ♗xc4 17. ♗xg7 ♘xd5 18. ♘xd5 (18. ♘h3 ♖g8) ♗xd5 19. ♗c3 ♗xa2 20. ♘h3 ♗d6 21. ♖d2 ♗e6 22. g4 h5 23. ♖g1 hxg4 24. fxg4 ♖g8 25. ♖dg2 ♗c5 26. ♘f2 ♗d5 0-1

White has a rook and a pawn for the knight, but Black's pieces dominate.

Ruofan Li – Hilton Bennett
Shenyang 1999

22...♗c5 23. ♕xd3 (23. ♕a4 ♗xe3 24. ♘c2 ♘ef2+ 25. ♖xf2 ♘xf2+ 26. ♔g1 ♗c5) ♘g3+ 24. hxg3 ♗xd3 25. ♗xc5 ♕xc5 26. ♖fd1 ♖d6 0-1

Here too, it is White's undeveloped pieces which are targeted.

Miroslav Maslik – Sergei Krivoshey
Presov 1997

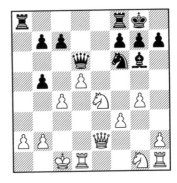

18...♘xe4 19. fxe4 ♕f4+ 20. ♖d2 ♕xe4, winning the h-rook 0-1

Next we have a fine example of the kind of piece cooperation that Black can enjoy in this opening.

Siniša Cucančić – Filip Ljubičić
Opatija 1999

18...♗xh2+ 19. ♔f2 (if 19. ♔xh2,

14

then 19...♖h6+ mates) 19...♖e6 20. g3 ♗xe2 21. ♖xe2 ♗xg3+:

22. ♔f1 ♕h4 23. ♖g2 ♕h1+ (23...♖fe8 is better) 24. ♖g1 ♕h3+ 25. ♖g2 ♖f6 26. ♔g1 ♖h6 0-1

White has an extra pawn and can afford to give it back (20. ♘e4), but his pieces are ill-placed to contain the attack regardless.

Luis Ucha – Francisco Restuccia
San Antonio de Padua 2001

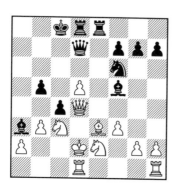

19...♘xd5 20. ♘xd5 (20. ♘e4 ♘xe3 21. ♕xd7+ ♗xd7 22. ♔xe3 f5) ♕xd5 21. ♕xd5 ♖xd5+ 22. ♘d4 ♗b2 23. bxc4 bxc4 24. ♖c1 c3+ 0-1

Let us examine the variations without 5. ♗b5+. In the next game, White plays c2-c4 early to protect the advanced d-pawn, and then trades the d5-pawn for Black's e6- and f7-pawns so he is now ahead by two. On the other hand, Black is fully developed and his pieces are active.

Gennady Sergeev – Dmitri Saulin
Tula 2005

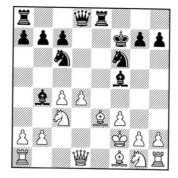

10...♖xe3 11. ♔xe3 ♗c2 12. ♕d2 (12. ♕xc2 ♕xd4+ 13. ♔e2 ♗xc3 14. bxc3 ♖e8+ 15. ♕e4) ♘g4+.

A remarkable position!

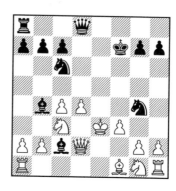

13. fxg4 (13. ♔e2 ♕e7+ 14. ♘e4 ♗xd2 15. ♔xd2 ♗xe4 16. fxg4 ♕b4+; 13. ♔f4 ♗d6+ 14. ♔xg4 ♗f5+ 15. ♔xf5 ♕h4) ♕g5+ 14. ♔f2 ♕xd2+ 0-1

A nearly identical opening: White plays c2-c4 and then trades his d-pawn for Black's e- and f-pawns. He has just played 11. ♘g3.

15

Pascal Horn – Fabrice Liardet
Geneva 1999

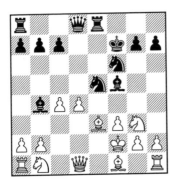

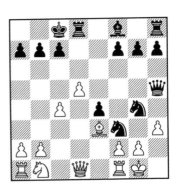

13. gxf3 ♘xe3 14. fxe3 ♕xh3 15. ♕e2 ♖d6 16. ♔f2 ♕h4+ 0-1

11...♘eg4+ 0-1 (also 11...♘fg4+, i.e. 12. fxg4 ♘xg4+ 13. ♔g1 ♘xe3 14. ♕h5+ ♔g8 15. ♘c3 ♕xd4 16. ♘b5 ♕b6 17. ♘e2 ♗g4)

Black enjoys a couple of pins: One is partly due to his quickly activated queen, and the other is a result of his opponent's undeveloped queen.

White has plenty of good targets. Here he punches through in the center, setting up a post for the knight.

Eberhard Simon – Ernst Fischer
Gladenbach 1999

Clive Wismayer – Paul Barnard
Guernsey 2001

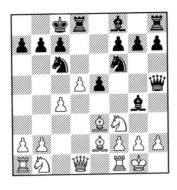

12. d5 exd5 13. cxd5 ♘b4 14. ♘e5 ♕f5 15. ♘xf7 ♗d6 16. ♘xd8 ♖xd8 17. ♘b5 ♘c2 18. ♗xa7+ ♔a8 19. ♘xd6 cxd6 20. ♗b6 ♖f8 21. ♖ac1 ♘b4 22. ♕e6 1-0

9...e4 10. ♘d4 ♘xd4 11. ♗xg4+ ♘xg4 12. h3 ♘f3+

The only move to keep the attack alive:

In the example that follows, the knights attack on the other wing.

John Littlewood – Edward Taylor
Liverpool 2006

11. ♘db5 ♕d7 (11...♕c5 12. ♘xd5 0-0-0 13. c4) 12. ♘xd5 ♘xd5 13. ♕xd5 ♕xd5 14. ♘xc7+ ♔d7 15. ♘xd5 ♗xc2 16. ♗f4 e6 17. ♗b5+ ♔d8 18. ♘c7 ♖c8 19. ♖c1 ♗e4 20. ♖d1+ ♔e7 21. ♗g5+ 1-0

The queen trap is a typical motif. Here, the black queen manages to get away, but at a steep price.

Nuutti Sorsa – Hannu Salmela
Jyväskylä 1998

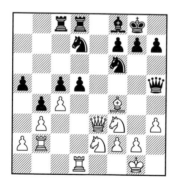

22. ♘g3 d4 23. ♕c1 ♕g6 24. ♘h4 1-0

In the game below, White reels in Her Majesty.

Daniel Paz Ladrón de Guevara –
Rodrigo Chaves Alcoba
Málaga 1999

19. g4 ♕e6 20. ♕d3 1-0 (20...♕f6 21. ♘e4 ♕e6 22. ♘fg5)

Two problems here: Castling into the pawn majority, and a queen lacking in mobility.

Monica Calzetta – Christophe
Philippe, Chambéry 2008

12. a3 exd4 (12...♗e7 13. b4) 13. axb4 ♕xb4 14. ♘xd4 ♘xd4 15. ♗xd4 a6 16. ♗c3 ♕c5 17. ♕c2 ♖he8 18. b4 ♕e7 19. ♗f3 ♕e6 20. ♗xf6 ♕xf6 21. b5 1-0

Puzzles

Now for some practice positions from Portuguese/Jadoul miniatures.

(Solutions on p. 111.)

Black to move:

Black to move:

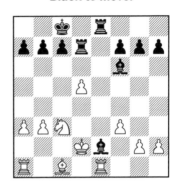

Black mates in 5:

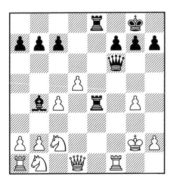

Black to move:

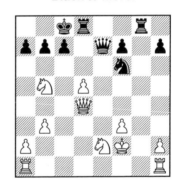

Black to move:

Black mates in three:

Black to move:

Black mates in four:

Black mates in three:

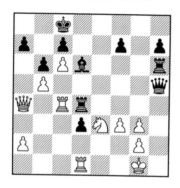

Black to move:

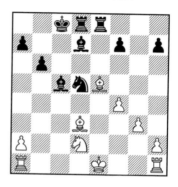

Black to move:

Black to move:

Black to move:

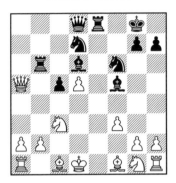

Black mates in two:

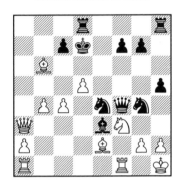

Black to move:

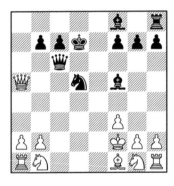

Black to move:

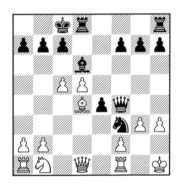

Black mates in two:

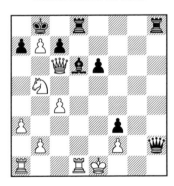

Black to move:

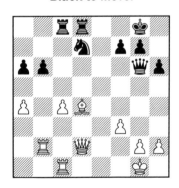

Black to move:

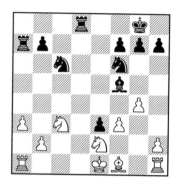

Black to move:

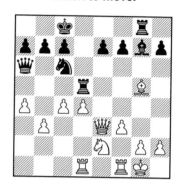

Black to move:

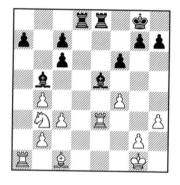

White to move:

Black to move:

White to move:

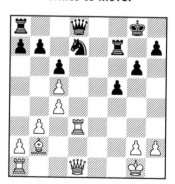

White mates in 5:

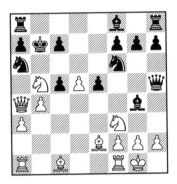

White to move:

White to move:

White mates in 5:

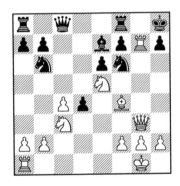

White to move:

White to move:

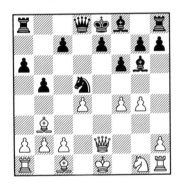

White to move:

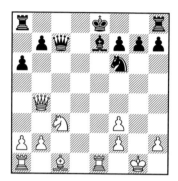

White to move:

Chapter 3

Caro-Kann Fantasy Variation (B12)

Our discussion of the Fantasy Variation centers around the gambit 1. e4 c6 2. d4 d5 3. f3 dxe4 4. fxe4 e5 5. ♘f3 exd4 6. ♗c4:

White gives up a pawn with the idea of attacking f7 with bishop and rook. The pawn on e4 can easily move in, while the queen deploys to b3 to provide assistance and attack Black's queenside. This is one of the more popular continuations in the Fantasy, the main diversions from this being the conservative defenses 3...e6 or 3...g6. The open f-file creates offensive possibilities, while less aggressive continuations are not harmless, as we shall see.

Black gains immediate counterplay in the following position:

Gilbert Temme – Stewart Schwartz
Ventura 1971

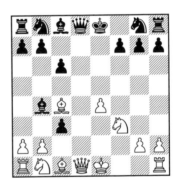

8. ♗xf7+ ♔xf7 (if 8...♔e7 9. ♕b3!)

Down a bishop and pawn, can White take the queen? If so, Black will get the a1-rook and queen the pawn:

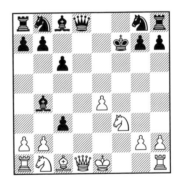

9. ♕xd8 cxb2+ 10. ♔e2 bxa1♕

24

White now mates in 5.

11. ♘g5+ ♔g6 12. ♕e8+ ♔h6 13. ♘e6+ ♗d2 14. ♗xd2+ g5 15. ♗xg5# 1-0

Once lines are opened to the enemy king, the defenses can be smashed.

Karel Hromádka – Josef Dobiáš
Plzeň 1911

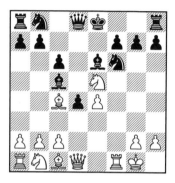

9. ♘xf7 ♔xf7 (9...♗xf7 10. ♗xf7+ ♔xf7 11. ♕h5+) 10. ♕h5+ ♔f8 11. ♗xe6 ♕e7 12. e5 (12. ♖xf6+ ♕xf6 13. ♕xc5+ is devastating) 12...♘a6 (better is 12... ♕xe6) 13. ♖xf6+:

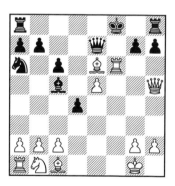

13...♕xf6 14. exf6 g6 15. ♕h6+ ♔e8 16. ♕g7 d3+ 17. ♔h1 d2 18. ♕d7+ 1-0

Jan Balin – Vojtech Kovar
Most 1999

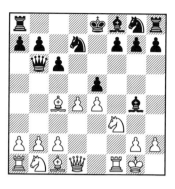

8. ♗xf7+ ♔d8 9. ♔h1 ♗xf3 10. ♕xf3 ♕xd4 11. ♖d1 ♕b4

White is all over the board:

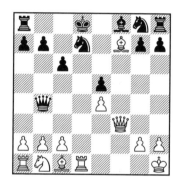

12. ♗xg8 ♖xg8 13. ♕f7 1-0

Below we watch what amounts to a dance between material and mobility.

Levin Naum – Machavariani
USSR 1971

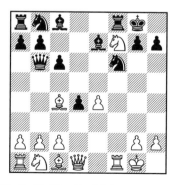

10. ♖xf6 d3+ 11. ♔h1:

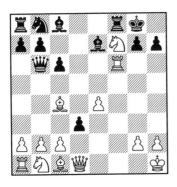

11...gxf6 (11...&xf6 12. ♕h5 ♕c7 13. ♘g5+; 11...dxc2 12. ♕h5 mates) 12. ♕h5 f5 13. ♘g5+ ♚g7 14. ♕xh7+ ♚f6 15. ♕h6+ ♚e5 16. ♘f3+ ♚xe4 17. ♘c3#

Mark Paragua – Aditya Prasetyo
Philadelphia 2000

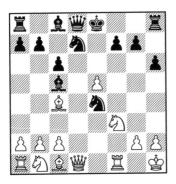

10. &xf7+ ♚e7 (10...♚xf7 11. ♘g5+ ♚g8 12. ♘xe4 ♕e7 13. ♘xc5 ♘xc5 14. ♕d6) 11. &g6 traps the knight:

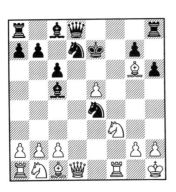

11...♘f2+ 12. ♖xf2 &xf2 13. ♕d6# 1-0

The next example illustrates the mate threat on f7.

José Sousa – Oscar Mendes
Porto 2000

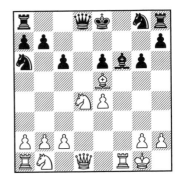

12. ♕f3 (the bishop is pinned) 12...♘b4 (12...♘c5 13. &xf6 ♕xf6 14. ♕xf6) 13. ♘a3 ♕xd4+ 14. &xd4 &xd4+ 15. ♚h1 0-0-0 16. c3 1-0

Ján Krajňák – P. Jusko
Slovakia 2001

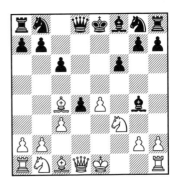

8. ♕b3 ♕e7 (better is 8...♘h6 9. ♕xb7 ♘d7 10. ♘xd4) 9. &xg8 ♖xg8 10. ♕xg8 ♕xe4+ 11. ♚f2 ♕c2+ 12. ♘bd2 ♘d7 13. ♖e1+ ♚d8 14. ♘xd4 1-0

Helgi Ziska – Christian Bleis
Copenhagen 2007

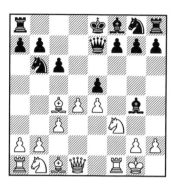

9. ♗xf7+ ♕xf7 (9...♔d8 10. ♗xg8 ♖xg8 11. ♕b3) 10. ♘xe5 ♗xd1 11. ♘xf7 ♗e2 12. ♖f2 ♗c4 13. ♘xh8 g6 14. ♘d2 ♗e6 15. ♘f3 ♘h6 16. ♘e5 ♘d7 17. ♘xd7 ♔xd7 18. ♘xg6 1-0

Michael Massoni – Andrey Grekh
Lvov 2009

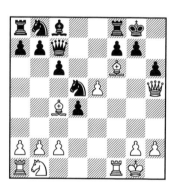

13. ♖f3 ♕a5 (13...gxf6 14. ♖g3+ ♔h7 15. ♗d3+) 14. ♖g3 ♕e1+ 15. ♗f1 1-0

There are other gambits beyond the 6. ♗c4 variation, including "poisoned pawn" lines. Black gets counterplay, but this can end badly.

Alexey Ivanov Jr. – Eduard Gorovykh
St. Petersburg 2007

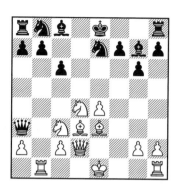

12. ♘cb5 ♕xa2 (12...cxb5 13. ♘xb5 ♗c3 14. ♘xc3 0-0 15. 0-0 ♘bc6 16. ♘b5 ♕a5 17. ♕xa5 ♘xa5 18. ♗c5 ♘ac6 19. ♘c7 ♖b8 20. ♘d5 ♖e8 21. ♗b5) 13. ♘d6+ ♔d7 14. 0-0 ♔xd6 (14...b6 15. ♘xf7 ♖f8 16. ♗c4 ♕a3 [16...♕xc4 17. ♘xc6+] 17. ♘b5+) 15. ♗c4:

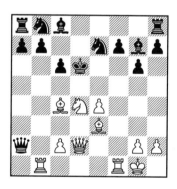

15...♕xc4 16. ♘b5+ ♔e5 17. ♕d6+ ♔xe4 18. ♕f4+ 1-0

Behold a series of forced exchanges:

Julian Hodgson – Maxwell Fuller
Novi Sad 1990

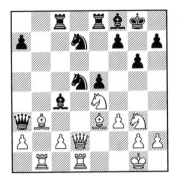

20. ♗xc4 ♕xe3+ 21. ♕xe3 ♘xe3 22. ♖xd7 ♘xc4 23. ♘f6+:

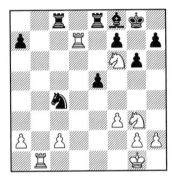

23...♔g7 24. ♘xe8+ ♖xe8 25. ♘e4 ♖e7 26. ♖xe7 ♗xe7 27. ♖b7 ♗d8 28. ♔f2 h6 29. ♔e2 ♗b6 30. g3 ♔f8 31. c3 ♘a5 32. ♖d7 ♘c4 33. ♔d3 ♘b2+ 34. ♔c2 ♘c4 35. ♔b3 ♘a5+ 36. ♔b4 f5 37. ♘d6 ♘c6+ 38. ♔b5 ♘e7 1-0

Alexey Ivanov Jr – Vasile Sanduleac
Bucharest 2007
White mates in four:

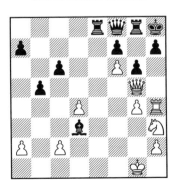

29. ♖xh7+ 1-0

R. Ligeti – Zsolt Timár
Hungary 1984

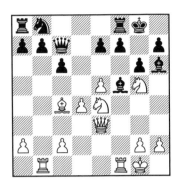

Black gives back the pawn, but White wins easily with the following sacrifice.

16. ♖xf5 gxf5 17. ♕h3 ♔g7 18. ♕xf5 ♗xg5 19. ♘xg5 1-0

How about a double rook offering? The Fantasy features that, too.

András Ozsváth – Luben Popov
Bulgaria 1971

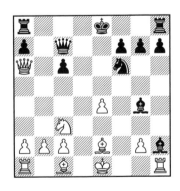

The position looks even, but then the fireworks begin:

13. ♖xh2 ♕xh2 14. ♕xc6+ ♔e7 15. ♗e3 ♕h1+ 16. ♔f2 ♕xa1

There it is! White mates in 7:

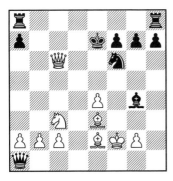

17. ♘d5+ ♘xd5 18. ♗c5+ ♔d8 19. ♕xd5+ ♗d7 20. ♗b5 ♕e1+ 21. ♔xe1 ♔c7 22. ♕xd7+ ♔b8 23. ♗d6# 1-0

This is a "gambit attack," as White offers material for a strong offensive.

Benoist Busson – Marco Rosso
Provence 2002

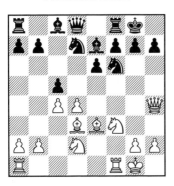

11...cxd4 12. ♗g5 g6 13. ♘e4 ♖e8 14. ♗xf6 ♗xf6 15. ♘fg5 ♗xg5 16. ♘xg5 ♘f6

Down a pair of pawns for several moves, White finally cashes in:

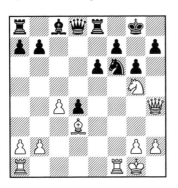

17. ♖xf6 ♕xf6 18. ♕xh7+ ♔f8 19. ♖f1 1-0

Tomasz Bohdanowicz – Marek Hałas
Wrocław 2005

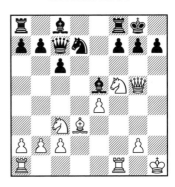

16. ♘h6+ ♔h8 17. ♘xf7+ ♔g8 18. ♘h6+ ♔h8 19. ♖xf8+ ♘xf8 20. ♕xe5 1-0:

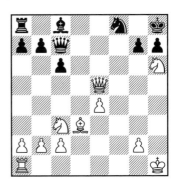

And now for a variation on the ♘xf7 theme.

Mikhail Antipov – Dmitry Ponomarev
Serpukhov 2009

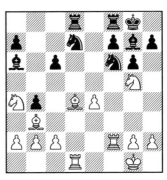

17. ♘xf7 ♖xf7 18. ♗xf6 1-0

Of course, Black can win in the Fantasy, too. Here is an opening pattern to avoid.

Esa Auvinen – Harri Hytönen
Helsinki 1993

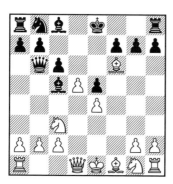

Black mates in two:

8...♗f2+ 0-1

White should castle before embarking on his attack.

Maxim Krupnov – Igor Sitnikov
Tula 2002

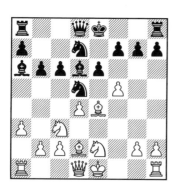

12...♘xc3 13. ♘xc3 ♕h4+ 0-1 (if 14.

g3, then 14...♗xg3+ mates)

Black, too, can use the open f-file.

Ignacio Ainsa Claver – Félix Izeta
Benasque 1996

15...♗c7 16. ♘ce2 0-0 0-1

In the following position, White has declined the poisoned pawn. With the dark-squared bishops off the board, Black's knights – the slowest pieces on the board – carry the field.

Frédéric Simon – Dragoş-Nicolae
Dumitrache, Avoine 2001

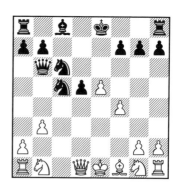

12...♘e4 13. ♕c2 (13. ♕e2 ♕d4) ♕e3+ 14. ♘e2 ♘b4 0-1

Puzzles

Some combinations exist because of the personality of the opening system. Here is an assortment of quick wins in the Fantasy. (Solutions on p. 117.)

White to move:

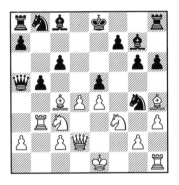

White to move:

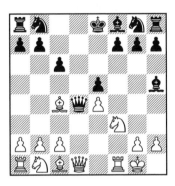

White to move:

Black mates in four:

White to move:

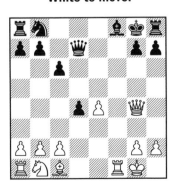

White to move:

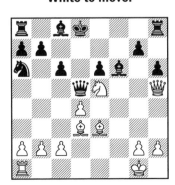

Black to move:

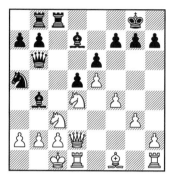

White to move:

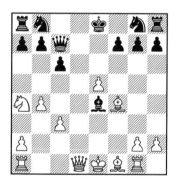

Black to move:

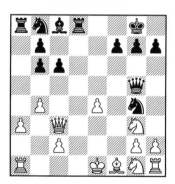

The Wing Gambit (B20)

In the Wing Gambit, White gives up a pawn, but it is only the b-pawn, a flank soldier. Because of this factor, this gambit differs from most of others: if Black decides to return the pawn, it will probably be a better pawn, in which case for all practical purposes the variation becomes a gambit by Black and not White.

The following five positions have been equally popular over time, and they represent the basic schemes for development in this opening.

A.
1. e4 c5 2. b4 cxb4 3. d4 d5 4. e5 ♘c6:

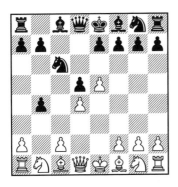

Black creates a wedge on b4 and sets the knight to guard it. White has created space in the center and already restricts Black's normal kingside deployment.

B.
1. e4 c5 2. b4 cxb4 3. a3 d5 4. exd5 ♛xd5 5. ♘f3 e5:

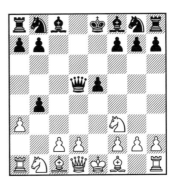

This is a more open, tactical game and the gambit status has not been resolved. If White develops carefully, then Black's queen is surely out of place in the center.

C.
1. e4 c5 2. b4 cxb4 3. a3 bxa3 4. ♘xa3:

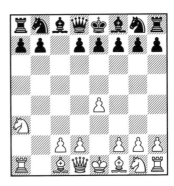

White has created the potential to attack both flanks. A double attack is worth the pawn invested. Where should Black put the king? The second player has moved but one pawn (which isn't even on the board anymore), and king safety is already at issue.

D.
1. e4 c5 2. b4 cxb4 3. a3 e6 4. axb4 ♗xb4 5. c3 ♗e7 6. d4:

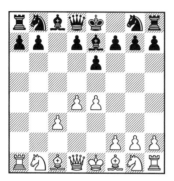

White has created the ideal pawn center and favorable attacking prospects on the queenside.

E.
1. e4 c5 2. b4 cxb4 3. ♗b2 d5 4. exd5 ♕xd5:

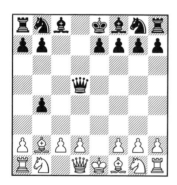

The black queen dominates the center, while the extra pawn prevents the move ♘b1-c3 that would drive her off d5. At the same time, White's bishop at b2 has a seemingly permanent fix on the enemy kingside. With normal development, Black will need to provide for the queen's safety, costing time.

Wins result from either of two major causes – poor development by the defender, or freely ranging pieces in the wing creating huge opportunities for the attacker. In the following example, White's queen takes in the entire board.

Thomas Wächter – Steffen Kästner Bonn-Röttgen 1999

6. ♗xf7+ ♔xf7 7. ♕h5+ g6 8. ♕d5+ e6 9. ♕xa8 ♕c7 10. ♖b1 ♘a6 11. ♖b7 ♕c6 12. ♕xa7 ♘f6 13. ♖b6 1-0

How important is the b-pawn? If White still had her b-pawn, the following move would not work.

Ekaterina Matseyko – Evgeniya Dolukhanova, Kiev 2002

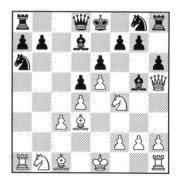

12. ♘g6 ♗xc1 (12...fxg6 13. ♗xg6+ ♔f8 14. ♗a3+ [no b-pawn] ♗e7 15.

Wf3+; 12...⬜h7 13. f4) 13. ♘xh8 ♕e7 14. ♘xf7 ♗c6 15. 0-0 ♗b2 16. ♖a2 1-0

White has a two-pawn deficit, but the knight gallops across the board to save the day. Is it due to Black's poor development, or does offering a gambit make you faster?

Juan Javier Unciti – Fernando Martín Sánchez, Madrid 2002

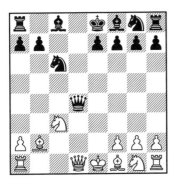

8. ♘d5 ♕xd1+ (8...♗g4 9. ♘c7+ ♚d8 10. ♗xd4 ♗xd1 11. ♘xa8) 9. ♖xd1 ♚d8 10. ♘b6+ ♚c7 11. ♘xa8+ ♚b8 12. ♘f3 f6 13. ♗b5 e5 14. 0-0 ♚xa8 15. ♗xc6 bxc6 16. ♖d8 ♘e7 17. ♖b1 g5 18. ♗a3 1-0

A pawn thrust can be let loose an enormous amount of energy.

Kevin Felczer – Thomas Pähtz Bad Bevensen 1994

14. d5 exd5 15. cxd5 (if 15...♘a5 16. d6) 1-0

White demonstrates that it is indeed possible to win by moving only pawns.

R. Kujoth – Fashing-Bauer Milwaukee 1950

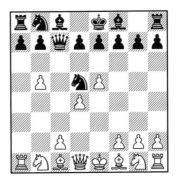

8. c4 ♘b6 9. c5 ♘d5 10. b6 1-0

In the following example, Black appears to have created a poisoned-pawn situation.

Roberto Bevilacqua – Guido Coppola Como 2000

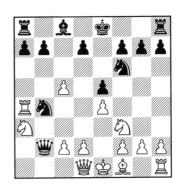

10. c3 d5 (10...♘c6 11. ♘c4) 11. cxb4 ♗d7 12. ♗b5 ♘xe4 13. ♗xd7+ ♚xd7 14. 0-0 ♖ae8 15. ♖e1 f6 16. ♖xe4 1-0

In the Wing Gambit, White's queenside seems to coordinate more easily when unencumbered by pawns.

David Lana Rodríguez – Francisco Labrador Postigo, Aragón 2005

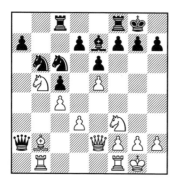

16. ♖a1 ♕b3 17. ♖a3 1-0

As the queen is exposed early on in some variations of the Wing, here is another example of trapping.

Luca Ronzano – Marco Crepaldi Asti 2006

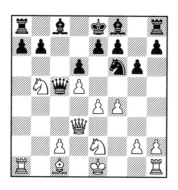

13. ♗e3 ♕b4+ 14. c3 ♕xe4 15. ♕xe4 ♘xe4 16. ♘c7+ ♔d8 17. ♘xa8 1-0

Black makes good use of the c-file in the game below.

Thomas Gietl – Gerd Fischer Bavaria 2006

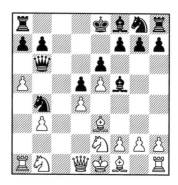

10...♕c7 (10...♕c6 11. ♘ec3 ♘c2+ 12. ♕xc2 ♗xc2 13. ♗b5) 11. ♘bc3 (11. ♔d2 ♕c2+ 12. ♕xc2 ♘xc2 13. ♖a2 ♘xe3) 11... ♗c2 0-1

Although White appears to dominate, Black can create dynamic play.

Hans Melters – Marcel May Cologne 1997

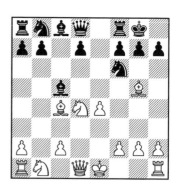

8...♕a5+ 9. ♗d2 (9. ♕d2 ♕xd2+ 10. ♘xd2 ♗xd4; 9.c3 ♗xd4 10.♕xd4 ♕xg5) 9...♕a4 10. ♗g5 ♘xe4 11. ♗xf7+ ♖xf7 0-1

Already down a pawn, White breaks the center open with a knight sacrifice and wins swiftly.

Daniel Capron – Jean Rabier
St-Chely d'Aubrac 2004

14. ♘d5 exd5 (14...♕d6 15. ♘xb4 ♕xb4 16. ♘xc6) 15. ♘xc6+ ♔f8 16. ♘xb4 ♘e7 1-0

The bishop fianchettoed on the gambited pawn's starting square yelds White long-distance mate threats.

Dietrich Klingenberg – Vladislav Frish
Greifswald 2003

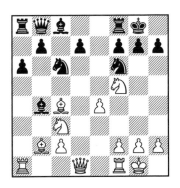

14. ♘d5 ♘xd5 (14...♘e8 15. ♕g4 ♘e5 16. ♕g5 ♔h8 17. ♘xb4) 15.♕g4 (checkmating) ♗c3 16. ♗xc3 1-0

Puzzles

(Solutions on p. 118.)

White mates in two:

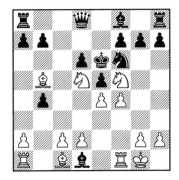

White mates in two:

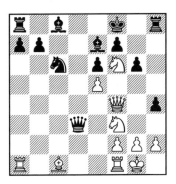

White mates in two:

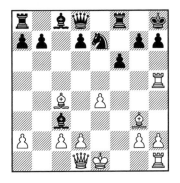

White to move:

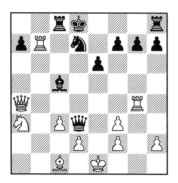

White to move:

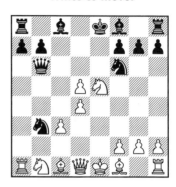

Black to move:

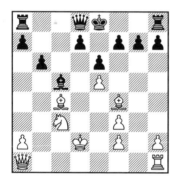

White to move:

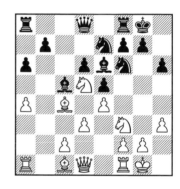

White to move:

White to move:

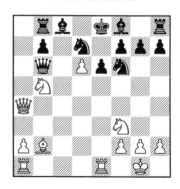

White to move:

Black to move:

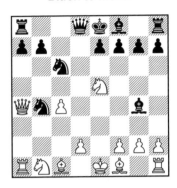

White to move:

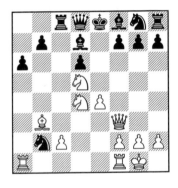

Black mates in 6:

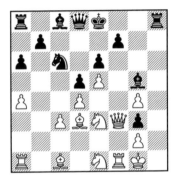

Black mates in 7:

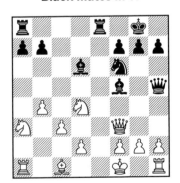

Chapter 5

Grand Prix Attack – Tal Gambit (B21)

There are four equally popular variations of the Tal Gambit, with some key differences.

1. e4 c5 2. f4 d5 3. exd5 ♘f6 4. ♗b5+ ♗d7 5. ♗xd7+ ♕xd7 6. c4 e6 7. ♕e2 ♗d6:

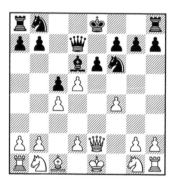

Black creates pressure on the d5-pawn, hoping for double isolated d-pawns once he is safely castled. White has a strong presence in the center for now, but lags in development and (in the case of d5xe6) is saddled with a backward d-pawn.

The game might also go 1. e4 c5 2. f4 d5 3. exd5 ♘f6 4. ♗b5+ ♘bd7 5. c4 a6 6. ♗xd7+:

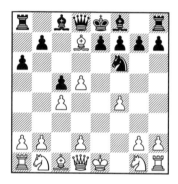

In this line Black possesses the bishop pair and, with the dark-squared bishop on g7, he enjoys ample counterplay in the center.

Alternatively, 1. e4 c5 2. f4 d5 3. exd5 ♘f6 4. c4 e6 5. dxe6 ♗xe6:

Black has free play and a lead in development.

1. e4 c5 2. f4 d5 3. exd5 ♘f6 4. ♘c3 ♘xd5:

In this variation, White gives back the material and solves the problem of the backward pawn. And yet... watch how easily Black capitalizes on the open space in the center and White's exposed pieces.

Odd Gunnar Malin – Svein Harald Johnsen, Vadsø 1998

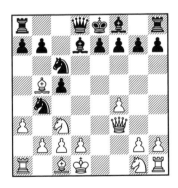

8...♘xc2 9. ♖b1 (9.♔xc2 ♘d4+) 9... ♗g4 0-1 (10. ♕xg4 ♘e3+)

White is up two bits, but they are weak. Black creates a diversion to leave the enemy royals further exposed.

Andrey Praslov – Tommy Indbryn Norway 1997

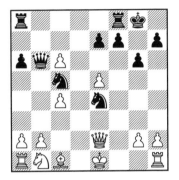

15...♘d3+ 16. ♔d1 (16. ♕xd3 ♕f2+ 17. ♔d1 ♖ad8 18. ♕d7; 16. ♔f1 ♘xc1 17. ♕xe4♕xb2)16...♘ef2+17.♔c2♘b4+18. ♔c3 ♘xh1 19. ♗e3 ♕a5 20. b3 ♕xe5+ 21. ♔xb4 ♕xa1 22. ♘c3 a5+ 0-1

Black makes an offer that his opponent cannot refuse, and White loses quickly.

Thomas Städele – Jens Ebeling Augsburg 1998

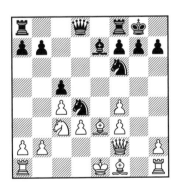

12...♘g4 13. fxg4 (13. ♕d2 ♘xf3+) 13...♕h4 14. ♗xd4 cxd4 15. ♘e4 ♗xf2+ 16. ♔xf2 ♕h4+ 17. ♔f3 f5 0-1

In the following position, White is down a pawn but controls key squares.

Jevgenyij Boguszlavszkij – Sándor Vidéki, Hungary 1997

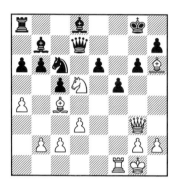

20. ♖xf5 ♗e7 21. ♘xb6 ♕d4+ 22. ♗e3 ♕d6 (22...♕xb2 23. ♗xe6+ ♔h8 24. ♘xa8 ♗xa8 25. ♖f1) 23. ♕xd6 ♗xd6 24. ♗xe6+ ♔h8 25. ♖d5 1-0

Black tries to trade queens, but White has a much better idea.

Miroslav Pfeifer – Petr Herejk Czech Republic 1996 White mates in 5:

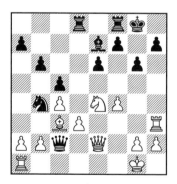

19. ♕h5 1-0

White seems to do well on Black's kingside. Below we see another effective sacrifice.

Martin Machata – Vladimir Harasta Bratislava 2001

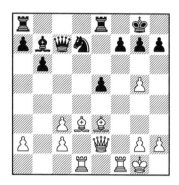

17. ♗xh7+ ♔xh7 (17...♔h8 18. ♕h5; 17... ♔f8 18. ♕h5 f6 19. gxf6 ♘xf6 20. ♖xf6+ gxf6 21. ♕g6 ♕f7 22. ♗h6+ ♔e7 23. ♖d7+) 18. ♕h5+ ♔g8 19. ♕xf7+ ♔h8 20. ♖xd7 1-0

Puzzles

Here is a sampler of tactical wins from the Tal Gambit. (Solutions on p. 121.)

White mates in four:

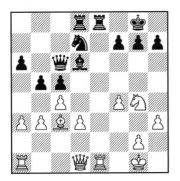

White to move:

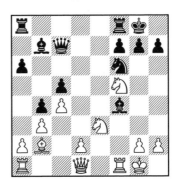

White mates in 5:

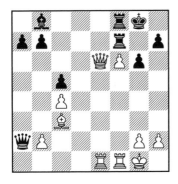

Black to move:

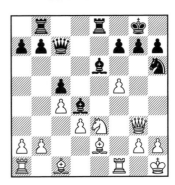

White to move:

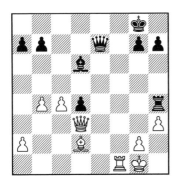

Black mates in 6:

Black to move:

Black mates in four:

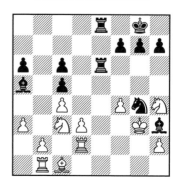

Black to move:

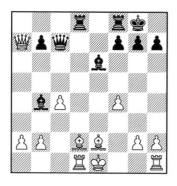

Black mates in four:

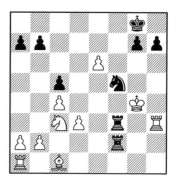

Chapter 6
French Defense – Milner-Barry Attack (C02)

Black's queen on b6 usually has an active hand in the Milner-Barry Attack from the French Advance variation. The gambit itself occurs in positions like the one below, which can be reached via numerous move-order transpositions. Black is up a pawn, but the queen takes the second pawn at e5. Tactical motifs abound in this variation.

1. e4 e6 2. d4 d5 3. e5 c5 4. c3 ♘c6 5. ♘f3 ♕b6 6. ♗d3 ♗d7 7. 0-0 cxd4 8. cxd4 ♘xd4 9. ♘xd4 ♕xd4:

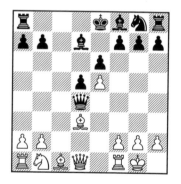

In the second variation, Black returns the pawn and prepares a queen-side attack in combination with a queen-plus-bishop battery on White's king at g1.

1. e4 e6 2. d4 d5 3. e5 c5 4. c3 ♘c6 5. ♘f3 ♕b6 6. ♗d3 ♗d7 7. dxc5 ♗xc5 8. 0-0 a5:

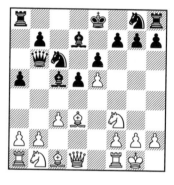

First into the field of battle, the queen takes more risks, so not surprisingly many of the tactics involve the queen. Sometimes just being on the wrong square creates opportunities.

Anton Schnurr – Hans Gerdes
Schloss Schney 1994

14. ♘b5 ♕a5 15. ♘d6+ 1-0

In the following gamer Black has an extra pawn, but the queen is trapped in the center of the board.

Peter Djurić – Božidar Jovičević
Igalo 1994

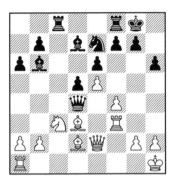

17. ♗e3 ♕b4 18. a3 ♕b3 19. ♗c2 1-0 (if 19...♕xb2 20.♗h7+)

Sometimes, shelter is but a cruel illusion.

Stephan Bardel – Cyprien Véron
Lyon 1990

11. ♗xf5 exf5 12. e6 ♗d6 13. exd7+ ♔xd7 14. 0-0 ♖he8 15. ♕d3 ♖e4 16. ♘bd2 1-0

If the Milner-Barry is built on the black queen's boldness, then it fol-lows that Black should be ever vigilant about her safety.

Jonas Ingvaldsen – Dag Andersen
Sarpsborg 2001

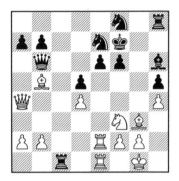

20. ♖xc1 ♗xc1 21. ♖c2 ♗h6 22. ♗c7 1-0

What about the king's own safety? This example concludes with a royal knight fork.

Ricardo Rubio Doblas – Máximo
Adrados Gil, Málaga 1999

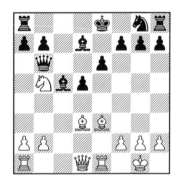

14. ♗xc5 ♕xc5 15. ♖c1 ♕b6 16. ♘c7+ ♔e7 (16...♔f8 17. ♘xa8 ♕xb2 18. ♖b1) 17. ♘xd5+ 1-0

The following position is a veritable mobile of hanging pieces. Black's protection is largely illusory.

Alberto Giménez Martínez – Pablo Aboy Nieto, Mondariz 2003

Michel Darras – Bertrand Rivet Herlies 2002

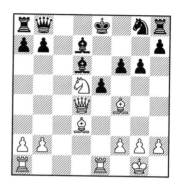

16. ♕g5 exd5 (16...f6 17. ♕xg7 ♘f7 18. ♘xf6+; 16...♗f6 17. ♘xf6+ gxf6 18. ♕xf6) 17. ♗xe5 ♕c8 18. ♗d6+ ♗e6 19. ♕e7# 1-0

16. ♘xf6+ ♘xf6 17. ♗xe5 ♗xe5 18. ♖xe5+ ♔d8 19. ♖e6 ♘e8 20. ♗b5 ♕c7 21. ♖d1 ♖f8 22. ♗xd7 1-0

In this game, the d-pawn can be taken with impunity with a discovered attack on the c-file, but first a little preparation is necessary.

Alexey Kislinsky – Vladimir Kovalenko Kiev 2001

16. ♗xh6 gxh6 17. ♘xd5 ♖xc1 (*Rybka* recommends 17...exd5) 18. ♘f6+ ♔e7 19. ♕xc1 ♕c6 20. ♕f4 1-0

Down a pawn, White sacs his knight.

Puzzles

Typical Milner-Barry themes can be seen in the positions that follow. (Solutions on p. 123.)

Black mates in two:

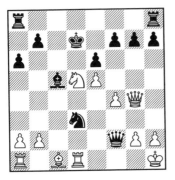

White to move:

White mates in three:

White to move:

Black mates in three:

White to move:

White to move:

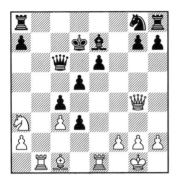

White to move:

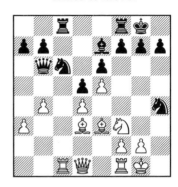

White to move:

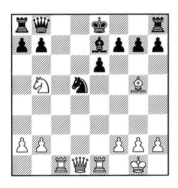

White to move:

White to move:

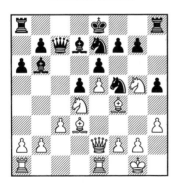

White to move:

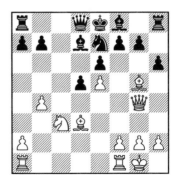

White to move:

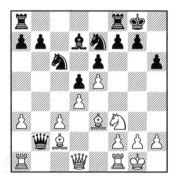

White to move:

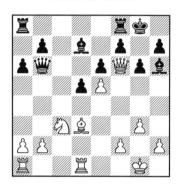

White mates in 5:

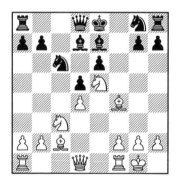

White mates in four:

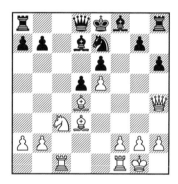

White mates in 5:

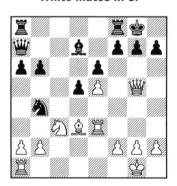

White to move:

White to move:

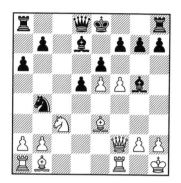

Black to move:

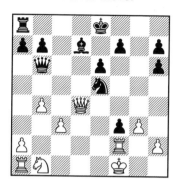

White to move:

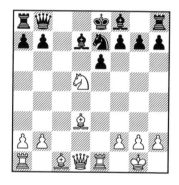

Black to move:

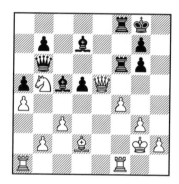

Chapter 7

The Rosentreter Gambit (C37)

Named after the German player, Adolf Rosentreter (1844-1920), this variation is part of the King's Gambit family. Unfortunately, only one of Rosentreter's games survives and it did not feature this line, so it is difficult to know much of its early development is actually due to Rosentreter. This not the opening for players who like to count material, as almost every variation contains an imbalance – an extra pawn, or two pawns for a knight.

The gambit begins with 1. e4 e5 2. f4 exf4 3. ♘f3 g5 4. d4. Black can roll his advanced pawn duo forward with 4...g4 5. ♗xf4 gxf3 6. ♕xf3 d5 7. exd5:

and then continue with 7...♘f6 followed with 8...♗g7, or vice versa. Black is a pawn's worth ahead in terms of material, but his position is slightly worse.

Black may opt to maintain the kingside tension and extend the pawn chain to three with 4...h6. Now White may continue with 5. h4 ♗g7 6. g3 d5, when Black appears to have both the pawn and control of the situation:

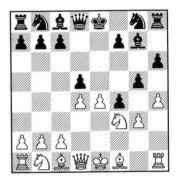

Alternatively, White can proceed less vigorously with 5. g3 fxg3 6. ♘c3 ♗g7 7. hxg3, and thereby maintain a slight edge according to *Rybka*:

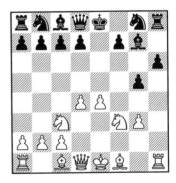

Typical middlegame features in this rare opening are the fractured pawns and the exposed kingside. Both sides have specific targets which, like shrapnel, are best avoided: There are more inviting targets beyond the loose pawns. There is a lot of piece play, and often both players' kings are vulnerable. Life expectancy is short for both sides in the Rosentreter.

In the following spectacular example, White is down a knight and his rook is under attack, yet he decides to sacrifice a bishop and, with mate in sight, also gives up a knight.

Igor Kan – Ilya Siomushkin
Kiev 2005

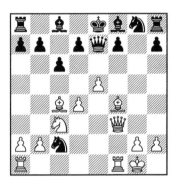

11. &g5 ♕xg5 (mate in 5) 12. ♕xf7+ ♔d8 13. ♕xf8+ ♔c7 14. ♘d5+:

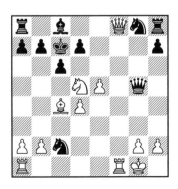

14...cxd5 15. ♕d6+ 1-0

White exploits the open files and semi-exposed king, and issues a decisive *Zwischenzug*.

Gilles Terreaux – Michael Harris
Internet 1993

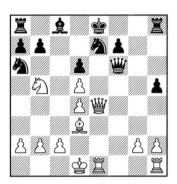

16. ♖hf1 &g4+ 17. ♔xg4 ♕xf1 18. ♕g7 ♕xe1+ 19. ♔xe1 ♘d7 20. ♕xf7:

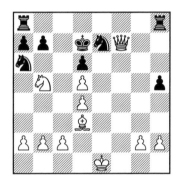

20...♖he8 21. ♕e6+ ♔d8 22. ♘xd6 (followed by 23. ♘xe8 or 23. &b5) 1-0

White gives up a pawn and wins a piece.

Víctor Acevedo – E. Arrúa
Asunción (Paraguay) 1989

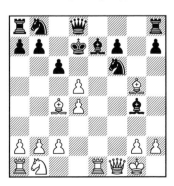

13. d6 ♔xd6 14. ♕f4+ ♔d7 15. ♗xf6 ♗xf6 16. ♕xg4+ ♔c7:

12. ♗xd6 ♗e5 13. ♗xf7+ ♕xf7 14. ♗xe5:

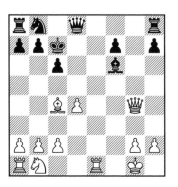

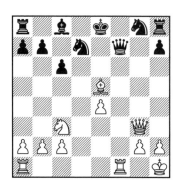

17. c3 ♖g8 18. ♕f4+ ♔c8 19. ♗xf7 ♖f8 20. ♗e6+ ♘d7 21. ♕d6 ♗e7 22. ♗xd7+ 1-0

In this game White may be down a knight, but his bishops make all the difference.

14...♘xe5 (14...♘gf6 15. ♗xf6 ♘xf6 16. ♕e5+ ♕e6 17. ♕xf6 ♕xf6 18. ♖xf6) 15. ♕xe5+ ♕e6 16. ♕xh8 ♗d7 17. ♕d4 b6 18. ♖ad1 0-0-0 19. ♕g7 ♘e7 20. ♖f8 ♖xf8 21. ♕xf8+ ♔b7 22. ♕g7 h5 23. h3 ♔a6 24. ♕g3 ♗c8 25. ♕d6 ♕f7 26. a4 ♗e6 27. b4 ♕f6 28. b5+ cxb5 29. ♘xb5 1-0

Vincenzo Menoni – Mario Fabbri
Bratto 1995

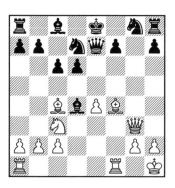

Puzzles

(Solutions on p. 127.)

White to move:

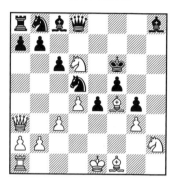

White mates in 6:

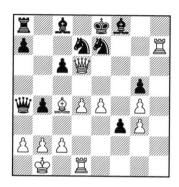

White to move:

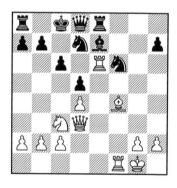

White mates in 6:

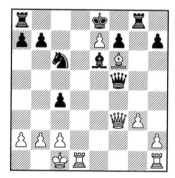

Chapter 8
Petroff's Defense – Cochrane's Gambit (C42)

This gambit line in the Petroff, or Russian Game, was introduced in an encounter between John Cochrane, one of the top players of his day, and Bannerjee in 1848. Cochrane was also linked to the Salvio Gambit. In the diagram below, a knight has been traded for two pawns.

1. e4 e5 2. ♘f3 ♘f6 3. ♘xe5 d6 4. ♘xf7 ♔xf7 5. d4

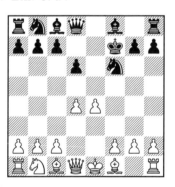

The e4-pawn is immune from capture, as ♕h5+ regains the material on e4:

Markus Hess – T. Born
Kirchheim 1990

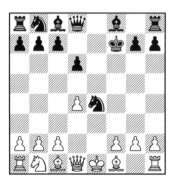

6. ♕h5+ ♔g8 (6...g6 7. ♕d5+ ♗e6 8. ♕xe4 is the usual continuation) 7. ♕d5+ mates 1-0

No other deviation from theory works:

Hannu Joentausta – Yrjö Siponen
Tampere 1992

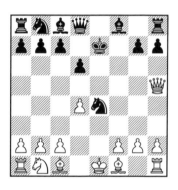

7. ♕e2 d5 8. ♗g5+ 1-0

The battle follows one of three main channels:

5...♗e7 6. ♘c3 ♖e8, preparing to castle by hand;

5...g6 6. ♘c3 ♗g7; preparing to fianchetto and create a flight square for the king;

5...c5 6. dxc5 ♘c6 7. ♗c4+, giving back the pawn.

In chess, as in karate, any force can be used against the opponent who wields it. The Cochrane has imbalances on several levels. An open position tends to favor the side with the "faster" pieces, and the more pieces a side has, the easier it is to trap an enemy unit. In the next example, the black queen attacks more squares than any other – and yet, she quickly gets trapped. This is conflict resolution.

Fernando Aller – Amador González de la Nava, Lisbon 2001

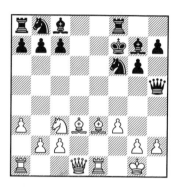

15. ♗c4+ ♗e6 16. ♗xe6+ ♔xe6 17. ♗g5+ ♔f7 18. h4 ♘c6 19. g4 ♖ad8 20. ♕e2 ♕xg5 21. ♕e6# 1-0

Clearly ♘e5xf7 works well with ♗f1-c4+, a theme also seen in the Fantasy and Scotch gambits. Here ♗f1-c4+ immobilizes Black's light-squared bishop.

Teemu Keskisarja – Antti Pihlajasalo Hyvinkää 1995

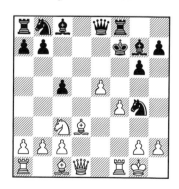

12. ♗c4+ (12. ♘b5 ♕c6 13. ♗c4+) ♗e6 (12...♔e7 13. ♕d6#) 13. ♘e4 ♔g8 14. ♘d6 1-0 (Δ 15. ♕xg4)

The position below features the c4-f7 diagonal loaded with chessmen, but with a potent threat. White plays a quiet move but it's the only winner.

Šarunas Šulskis – Thomas Michalczak Warsaw 2005

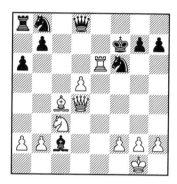

17. d6 ♔f8 18. ♘d5 (18. d7 followed by ♕c5+ or ♕d6+) ♘c6 19. ♕f4 ♗g6 20. ♘xf6 gxf6 21. ♕h6+ 1-0

In this diagram, Black has protected against the ♗c4+ motif, but White prepares a discovered attack on the black queen that quickly yields him a material edge.

Marion Albert – C. Köhler Rheinland-Pfalz 1991

13. 0-0-0 ♘xe5 (13...♗e6 14. ♗xh7+; 13...♖f8 14. ♕e4 ♗f5 15. ♕xf5 ♖xf5 16. ♗xf5 ♕f8 17. ♗xg4) 14. ♗xh7+ ♔xh7 15. ♕h5+ ♔g8 16. ♖xd8 ♖xd817. ♕xe5 ♘c6 18. ♕e4 ♗f6 19. ♘d5 1-0

Puzzles

Now for several more combinations arising from the Cochrane Gambit which, though outside the typical themes, are still useful in developing an understanding of this opening. (Solutions on p. 128.)

White to move:

White to move:

White to move:

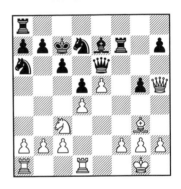

White mates in 5:

White to move:

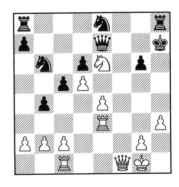

The Scotch Gambit (C44)

The Scotch Gambit arises after 1. e4 e5 2. ♘f3 ♘c6 3. d4 exd4 4. ♗c4:

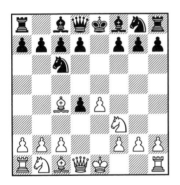

Black can meet this with 4...♘f6 5. 0-0 and continue either with 5...♘xe4 6. ♖e1 d5 7. ♗xd5 ♕xd5 8. ♘c3:

or with 5. e5 d5 6. ♗b5 ♘e4 7. ♘xd4 ♗d7:

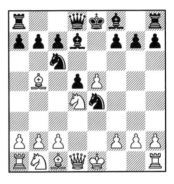

He can also try to hold the pawn with 4... ♗c5 5. c3:

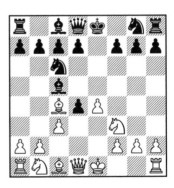

and then 5...♘f6, 5...dxc4, or even 5...d3. It's a wide-open game where the pieces coordinate well.

Our first example demonstrates Black's special vulnerability at f7.

Black has just retreated the bishop to e7 from b4 (better is 6...♗d6, with equal play).

W. Schachtler – Hubert Grabowski
Badenweiler 1985

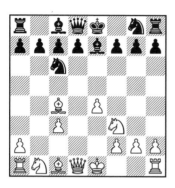

7. ♕d5 d6 (7...♘h6 loses quickly) 8. ♕xf7+ ♔d7 9. ♗e6# 1-0

Now for a slight variation on the same theme:

Mariusz Wajda – Mieczysław Morasiewicz, Polanica Zdrój 2008

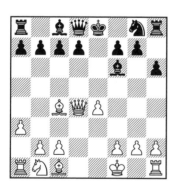

9. e5 1-0 (9...♗g5 10. ♕d5 ♕e7 11. f4)

The queen-plus-bishop attack on f7 need not be a death sentence. Contra-ry to popular wisdom, you can castle into the storm.

Rudolf Marić – Dragoljub Janošević
Zagreb 1953

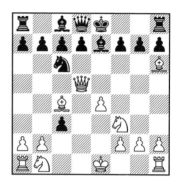

The game continued 7...0-0 8. ♗c1 (8. ♗xg7 is probably better) ♘b4 9. ♕h5 (9. ♕d1 c2 10. ♕d2 cxb1♕ 11. ♖xb1 d5 12. ♗xd5 ♘xd5) d5 10. exd5 ♘c2+ 11. ♔d1 ♘xa1 12. ♘xc3 ♗f6. Remarkably, Black has no worries in the resulting position:

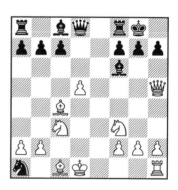

Here is another ♗xf7+ attack. White's pieces work together well to achieve domination.

**Iván Díaz – Juan José Sáenz
Oropesa 1996**

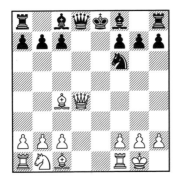

9. ♗xf7+ 1-0 (9...♔e7 10. ♖e1+)

In the following position, White can either equalize, or sacrifice in pursuit of victory.

**Zoltán Szabó – László Schmikli
Hungary 1993**

12. ♗xf7+ 1-0 (12...♔e7 13. ♗xg5+)

Now for an early example of the treatment of this opening. White can post a knight on d5 effectively. Although White is down two pawns, *Rybka* rates White up the equivalent of two. The pieces are well coordinated and radiate energy.

**Howard Staunton – Hugh Brodie
London 1851**

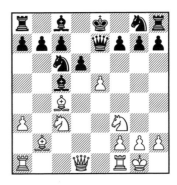

11. ♘d5 ♕d8 12. exd6 ♗xd6 13. ♗xg7 ♗g4 14. ♖e1+ ♘ge7 15. ♘f6# 1-0

In the following example, it is the f-rook which is forced to protect f7. A kingside attack ensues.

**Christophe Rousselet – Abdelhafid
Elamri, Paris 1999**

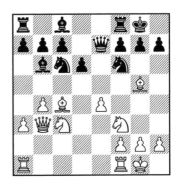

12. ♘d5 ♕d8 13. ♘xf6+ gxf6 14. ♗h6 ♘e5 15. ♘xe5 1-0

Another theme is introduced in the game below with ♕d1-h5. The queen's entrance ties together the action of the rook, bishop, and knight.

Maarten Westerweele – F. Rikumahu
Vlissingen 2000

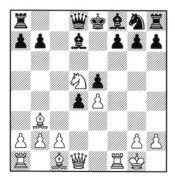

12. ♕h5 ♗e6 13. ♗a4+ 1-0

White can also use ♕d1-h5 for double attacks in the Scotch Gambit.

Čedomir Mičić – B. Pillotelle
Dortmund 1988

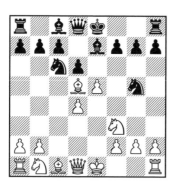

9. ♘xg5 ♗xg5 10. ♕h5 g6 11. ♗xc6+ bxc6 12. ♕xg5 1-0

In the next diagram we have a characteristic Scotch gambit conversion. The bishop at c5 is vulnerable, and White dispatches it.

Anna-Christina Kopinits – Anne Kast
Söchau 2000

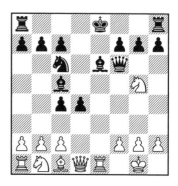

10. ♘xe6 fxe6 11. ♕h5+ g6 12. ♕xc5 ♖f8 13. f3 0-0-0 14. ♗g5 1-0

The queen on h5 attacks all: the f7- and h7-pawns, the king at e8, a minor piece at g5, and even the bishop at c5. The queen works well in an open board with any other piece.

In the position that follows, Black is on the counterattack. The knight posted at e4 dares the f3-pawn to push forward, inviting the queen to h4. Note the placement of Black's light-squared bishop, which has seized the critical diagonal leading down to f1.

Emil Aho – Peter Schütz
Budapest 2006

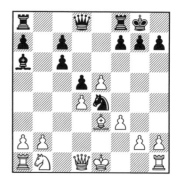

12...♕h4+ 13. g3 ♘xg3 14. ♗f2 ♕h3 (14...♕h6 15. ♗xg3 ♕e3+ mates) 15. ♖g1 ♘e2 0-1

Here is a similar counterthrust. Black's bishop provides the finishing touch.

A. Skjelde – Kjell-Arne Mork
Norway 1990

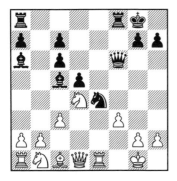

13...♕h4 14. fxe4 (better is 14. ♗e3 ♗d6 15. f4 ♗xf4 16. ♕f2+) 14...♗d6 (14...♕f2+ 15. ♔h1 ♗f1 mates) 15. h3 ♕f2+ 16. ♔h1 ♗f1 0-1:

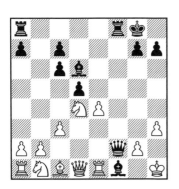

The move ...♕d8-h4+ is a recurring theme when breaking the gambit.

Nicholas Tavoularis – John Naylor
England 2007

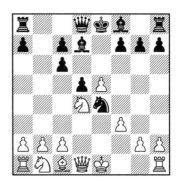

9...♕h4+ 10. ♔e2 ♕f2+ 11. ♔d3 c5 12. fxe4 ♕xd4+ 13. ♔e2 ♗g4+ 0-1

Below we have another win for Black featuring ...♕h4:

Maria Franzenburg – Anita Neldner
Halle 2005

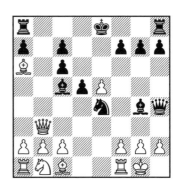

12...♗xf2+ 13. ♔h1 ♘g3+ 0-1

Though down in material, Black is ahead six pawns' worth according to *Rybka*:

Bob Romijn – Frans L. Arp
Amsterdam 1996

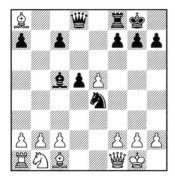

12...♗xf2+ 13. ♔h1 ♛h4 14. ♗f4 (14. g3 ♘xg3+) 14...♛xf4 15. g3 ♛f3+ 0-1

The f-pawn can be misplaced at f4 in addition to f3:

Kris Gibson – John Klukow
Winnipeg 2000

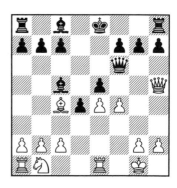

11...♛xf4 12. ♖f1 d3+ and mates 0-1

Jacek Tomczak – Dawid Królewicz
Krynica 1998

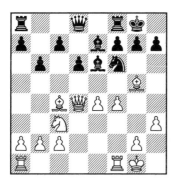

11...d5 12. ♛d3 (12. exd5 ♗c5) 12... dxc4 13. ♛e2 h6 14. ♗xf6 ♗xf6 15. e5 ♗e7 0-1

White has just played f2-f4 in the vain hope of opening the file with advantage:

Puzzles

The Scotch Gambit features numerous sacrifices and combinations that defy attempts at classification. (Solutions on p. 129.)

White to move:

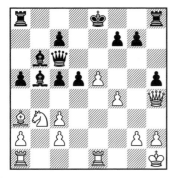

Black to move:

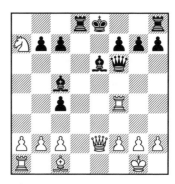

White to move:

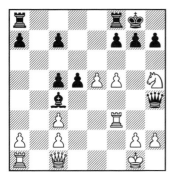

Black to move:

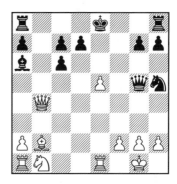

White to move:

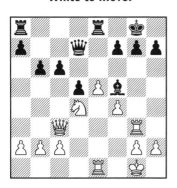

Black to move:

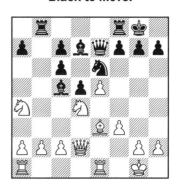

Black mates in four:

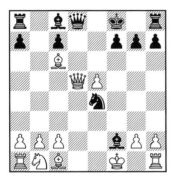

Black to move:

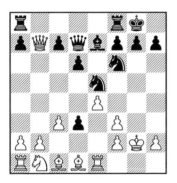

Black mates in four:

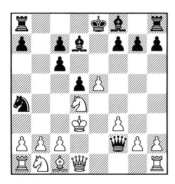

Chapter 10

Ruy López – Gajewski Gambit (C96)

This gambit was first played in a 2007 encounter between Viktor Kuznetsov and Polish grandmaster Grzegorz Gajewski: 1. e4 e5 2. ♘f3 ♘c6 3. ♗b5 a6 4. ♗a4 ♘f6 5. O-O ♗e7 6. ♖e1 b5 7. ♗b3 d6 8. c3 O-O 9. h3 ♘a5 10. ♗c2 d5:

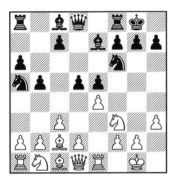

Since then, the line has been played by dozens of GMs – Lékó, Carlsen, Fressinet, Wojtaszek, and Benjamin, among others. White has replied in a variety of ways; the Gajewski's debut featured the most dynamic variation:

A.
   11. exd5 e4 12. ♘g5 ♘xd5 13. ♘xe4 f5 14. ♘g3 f4 15. ♘e4 f3:

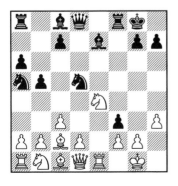

Black has created avenues of attack for most of his army and his f-pawn has made a dash for his opponent's kingside, where it will pry it open. White has but one active piece, which restricts the scope of two semi-mobilized pieces.

Rather than dance with his knight, White can opt for a quieter variation.

B.
   12. ♗xe4 ♘xe4 13. ♖xe4 ♗b7 14. d4 ♗xd5 15. ♖e1:

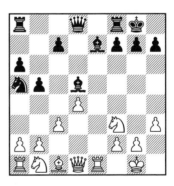

White is better developed than in the previous line, and now Black's knight looks awkwardly placed. White is up a pawn, but he has no ready targets.

The following two variations are fairly common, but they are not gambits and might be considered drawish since queens and rooks are traded early on. Still, they can be highly charged in their own right.

C.

11. d4 dxe4 12. ♘xe5 c5 13. ♗e3 ♗b7:

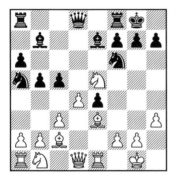

D.

11. d3 dxe4 12. dxe4 ♕xd1 13. ♖xd1:

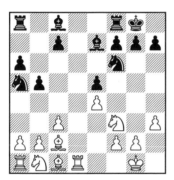

The Gajewski could be described as a delayed Marshall Attack. What are the implications? The main-line Marshall goes 8....d5 9. exd5 ♘xd5 10. ♘xe5 ♘xe5 11. ♖xe5:

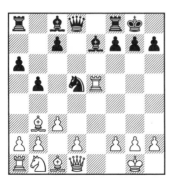

In the Gajewski, the a5-knight hinders the deployment of White's light-squared bishop to the dangerous b3-g8 diagonal, and – especially in variations B and C – opens to Black's light-squared bishop the long diagonal leading into White's castled position. Curiously, the knight is sometimes gambited itself. For example, in Volokitin – Wojtaszek, Heraklio 2007, the a5-knight was en prise to the b4-pawn for nine moves! Black's kingside attack was so strong that taking the knight was out of the question. This is the position after 19. b4:

19...f4 20. ♘f1 f3 21. gxf3 e3:

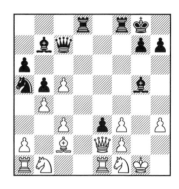

22. fxe3 (22. bxa5 exf2+ 23. ♕xf2 ♖xf3 24. ♕e2 ♖g3+ 25. ♘xg3 ♕xg3+ 26. ♔f1 ♕xh3+ 27. ♔g1 ♕h1+ 28. ♔f2 ♕g2#) 22...♖xf3 23. e4 (23. bxa5 ♖g3+ 24. ♘xg3 ♕xg3+) 23... ♖df8:

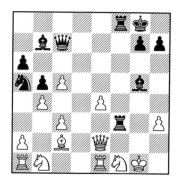

24. ♕g2 (24. bxa5 ♗h4 25. ♖c1 ♗f2+
26. ♕xf2 ♖xf2 27. ♘bd2 ♖xd2 28. ♗b3+
♔h8 29. ♘xd2 ♕g3+) 24...♗h4 (24...
♕f4 25. ♘bd2 ♖f2) 25. ♘bd2 ♖xc3 26.
♖ec1 ♗c8 27. bxa5 ♕xc5+ 28. ♔h1 ♖f2
29. ♗b3+ ♔h8 30. ♖xc3 ♕xc3 31. ♕xf2
♗xf2 32. ♖d1 ♗xh3 33. ♘h2 ♕g3 0-1

This stratagem occurs in identical positions in Caruana – Aveskulov, Plovdiv 2008, and Kravtsiv – Brkić, Gaziantep 2008:

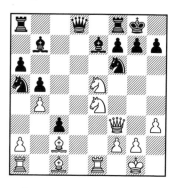

16...♘xe4 17. ♗xe4 ♗xe4 18. ♕xe4 f5 19. ♕b1 c2 20. ♕b2 ♘c4, when the knight was left hanging for four moves while taking care of other business.

These examples with the a5-knight hanging come from Variation C above (11. d4) and are very lively. In Nyysti – Nyback, Mantta 2008, the knight remained en prise on b4 to the c3-pawn for four moves.

Let us examine other dynamic positions from this young gambit. The following position is derived from Variation A. White's lack of development is only too clear. Black leads off with a large sacrifice.

**Ljuboje Bekić – Dagur Arngrimsson
Obrenovac 2008**

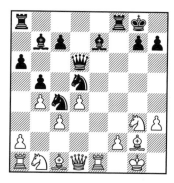

20...♖xf2 21. ♔xf2 (21. ♘e4 ♖xg2+
22. ♔xg2 ♘de3+ 23. ♗xe3 ♗xe4+)
♖f8+:

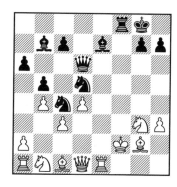

22. ♔g1 (22. ♘f5 ♖xf5+ 23. ♔g1 ♕g3
24. ♖xe7 ♘xe7 25. ♕e2 ♗xg2 26. ♕xg2
♕e1+ 27. ♔h2 ♖f2; 22. ♗f3 ♘xc3 23.
♕d3 [23. ♘xc3 ♗h4 24. ♖e5 ♗xf3 25.
♕xf3 ♕xd4+ 26. ♖e3 ♖xf3+ 27. ♔xf3
♗xg3] ♗h4 24. ♖g1 ♗xg3+ 25. ♖xg3
[25. ♔g2 ♗h4 26. ♗d5+] ♘e4+) 22...
♕xg3 23. ♖f1 ♘de3 24. ♖xf8+ ♗xf8 25.
♕e2 ♗xg2 26. ♕f2 ♕xh3 0-1

The attack below is relatively common in the Gajewski Gambit. As noted above, it can be argued that placing the knight on a5 clears the a8-h1 diagonal and enables Black's light-squared bishop to attack at a moment's notice.

Sara Jaćimović – Regina Pokorna
Rijeka 2009

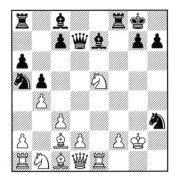

20...♖xf2+ 21. ♔h1 ♗b7+ (21...♗d8) 22. ♗e4 ♗xe4+ 23. ♖xe4 ♕f5:

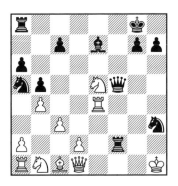

24. ♖e1 (24. ♕g4 ♖f1+ 25. ♔h2 ♖h1+ 26. ♔xh1 ♘f2+) ♕f4 25. ♘f3
(25. ♘g4 ♕g3) ♗d6 0-1

There is a great number of hanging pieces in the following game, also stemming from Variation A. How is it possible for White to go nineteen moves and move hardly any pieces off the first rank?

Leon Mazi – Manfred Freitag
Austria 2009

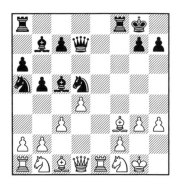

19...♘xc3 20. ♗g4 (20. bxc3 ♗xf3 threatening 21...♕xh3) ♕c6 21. ♗e6+ (21. d5 ♗xf2+ 22. ♔h2 ♘xd1 23. dxc6 ♗xe1 24. cxb7 ♘xb7) ♔h8 22. d5:

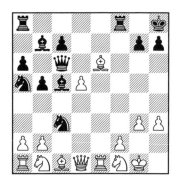

22...♗xf2+ (22...♕xe6 23. ♖xe6 [23. dxe6 ♖xf2 24. ♘e3 ♖g2+ 25. ♔h1 ♗xe3 26. ♕f3 {26. ♗xe3 ♘xd1}] ♗xf2+ 24. ♔h2 ♘xd1) 23. ♔h2 ♘xd1 24. dxc6 ♗xe1 25. cxb7 ♖ae8 26. ♗d7 ♖e2+ 27. ♔g1 ♗f2+ 28. ♔h1 ♗a7 29. ♗f4 ♘f2+ 30. ♔g2 ♘d3+ 31. ♔f3 ♖f2+ 32. ♔e4 ♘c5+ 33. ♔d4 0-1

The Gajewski has attracted the attention of some of the world's top players. It offers an abundant new source of tactics for the Ruy specialist to master. The line has performed well for Black, but White can play it profitably too.

Puzzles

Black to move:

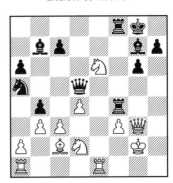

The process of learning of any opening can benefit from examining the typical tactics that feature in it. As with the other chapters, the following is not meant as an exhaustive compendium, but rather as an overview of the kinds of positions and the types of weaknesses to be found in this variation. Black is the one offering the gambit, however, so his/her tactics have to be the most telling. (Solutions on p. 134.)

Black to move:

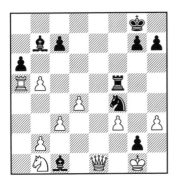

Black to move:

Black to move:

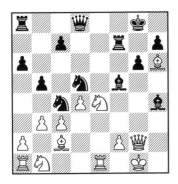

Black to move:

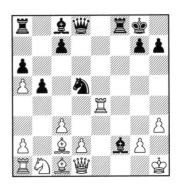

White to move:

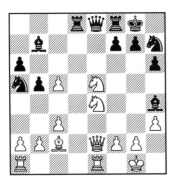

White to move:

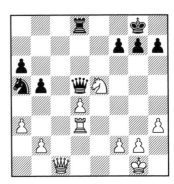

White to move:

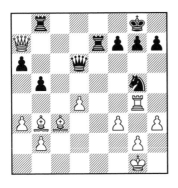

White to move:

White to move:

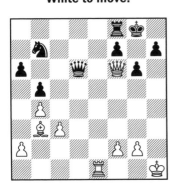

White to move:

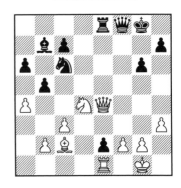

The Albin Countergambit (D08)

Black gives a pawn for the spike in the center:

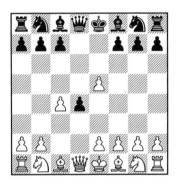

There are few transpositional possibilities in this opening, and the two main lines run as follows:

1. d4 d5 2. c4 e5 3. dxe5 d4 4. ♘f3 ♘c6 5. g3 ♗g4 6. ♗g2 ♕d7 7. 0-0 0-0-0:

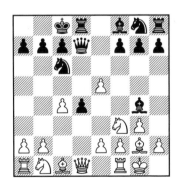

Or –
1. d4 d5 2. c4 e5 3. dxe5 d4 4. ♘f3 ♘c6 5. g3 ♗e6 6. ♘bd2 ♕d7 7. ♗g2:

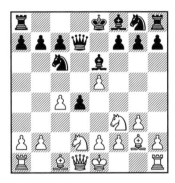

As this is Black's gambit, let's examine the wins by Black first. In this opening, Black's strategy centers around the d-pawn. It serves as a spearhead in White's territory, and Black aims to support it for a further advance protected by the mobile knight on c6 instead of a fixed pawn on c5, while a queen-plus-rook battery often lines up behind it. The d-pawn is the protagonist in our first example:

**Maria Kursova – Tatiana Kosintseva
Marina d'Or 1998**

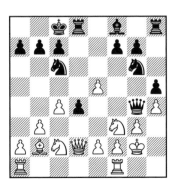

14...d3 15. ♘cd4 (15. exd3 ♖xd3 16. ♕xd3 ♘f4+; 15. ♘e3 dxe2 16. ♘xg4 exf1♕+ 17. ♖xf1 ♖xd2 18. ♘xd2 hxg4; 15. ♘h2 ♘xh4+ 16. ♔h1 ♕e4+ 17. f3 ♕xe2 18. ♕xe2 dxe2 19. ♖fe1 ♘f5 20. ♔g2 ♖d2 21. ♖ac1 ♖xc2) dxe2 16. ♖fc1 ♘xd4 0-1

In the second example, White's f-pawn is no support for the one at e3. White must abandon the queenside and lose the game.

Udo Hochstein – Hans-Georg Müller
Bochum 1991

13...dxe3 14. ♕xe3 (14. fxe3 ♕g3#; 14. ♘f3 exf2+ mates) ♕xb2 15. hxg4 ♕xa1+ 16. ♔e2 ♗a3 17. ♔f3 ♗c1 18. ♗d3 ♗xd2 19. ♖xa1 ♗xe3 0-1

Now for a comical situation: White is ahead a piece for the pawn and Black is about to promote, but only a knight will do. Imagine promoting a pawn on move 7!

William Wright – Ronald Finegold
Detroit 1990

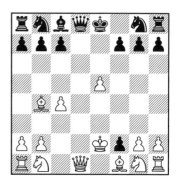

7...fxg1♘+ 8. ♔e1 ♕h4+ 9. ♔d2 ♘c6 10. ♗c3 ♗g4 11. ♕e1 0-0-0+ 12. ♔e3 ♕g5+ 13. ♔f2 ♖d1 14. ♕e4 ♗f5 15. ♕e3 ♖xf1+ 0-1

In the game below the d-pawn breaks into the king's castle with a discovered attack on the queenside.

Mark Abbott – Philip Bonafont
Yeovil 2009

17...♕f5 18. ♗g2 ♗xg2 19. ♔xg2 dxe3 0-1

The Albin is a dynamic game: there are plenty of tactics involving the major pieces.

Holger Dietz – Gábor Kádas
Kecskemét 1987

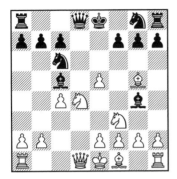

8...♕xg5 9. ♘xc6 (9. ♘xg5 ♗b4+ 10. ♕d2 ♗xd2+ 11. ♔xd2 ♘xd4) ♗xf3 10. gxf3 bxc6 0-1

Next there is another opening trap, a mere six moves into the game.

Teodoro Asensio Liñán – Joan Fluvià
Frigola, Catalonia 2000

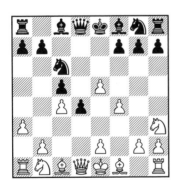

6...♗xh3 7. gxh3 ♕h4+ 8. ♔d2 ♕xf4+ 9. ♔e1 ♕h4+ 10. ♔d2 ♕e4 11. ♕c2 ♕xh1 12. ♕f5 g6 13. ♕f2 ♗h6+ 14. ♔c2 0-1

This position is only eight moves in, and White is already a sitting duck.

H. Reintjens – M. Bremers
Heerlen 1999

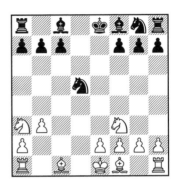

8...♗b4+ 9. ♘d2 ♗c3 10. ♖b1 ♗f5 11. ♘b5 ♗xd2+ 12. ♗xd2 ♗xb1 13. e3 ♘ge7 14. ♗c4 a6 15. ♘c3 ♘xc3 16. ♗xc3 0-0 17. ♗b4 ♖fe8 18. ♔e2 0-1

Black is down a piece, but he happily sacrifices the queen.

G. Requera – Leontxo García
Benidorm 1983

15...♕xf2+ (if 16. ♔xf2 ♗c5#) 0-1

Now for a win by White. He wraps a mating threat, an attack on the queen, and a double rook fork all in the same move.

Marc Lacrosse – Jean-Louis Guilbert
Le Touquet 1992

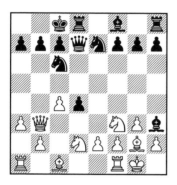

12. ♘e5 ♕f5 13. ♗xh3 ♕xh3 14. ♘xf7 d3 15. ♘xd8 ♘xd8 16. ♕xd3 h5 17. ♘f3 h4 18. ♖d1 ♘e6 19. ♕d7+ 1-0

White employs a similar strategy in the following position:

Jim Plaskett – Poul Rewitz
Esbjerg 1982

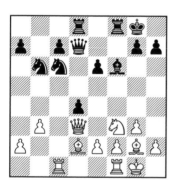

19. ♖xc6 1-0 (19...♕xc6 20. ♘g5)

Black has just recovered the pawn, and now it is White's turn to sacrifice.

Petri Kekki – Georg Osterman
Helsinki 1983

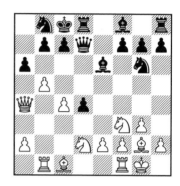

14. ♘xd4 ♕xd4 (14...♗g4 15. ♘c6 bxc6 16. bxa6 ♗c5 17. a7; 14...♘e5 15. ♘xe6 fxe6 16. ♕a5 ♕d4 17. ♗xb7+ ♔xb7 18. bxa6+) 15. bxa6 1-0 (15... bxa6 16. ♗b7#)

Puzzles

Supplementary critical positions from the Albin Countergambit. (Solutions on p. 136):

Black mates in four:

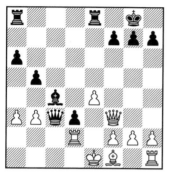

Black mates in four:

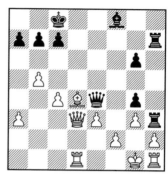

Black mates in three:

Black mates in 5:

Black mates in four:

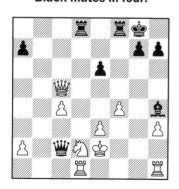

Black to move:

77

Black to move:

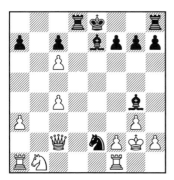

Black to move:

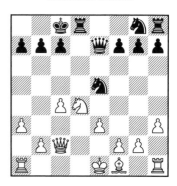

Black to move:

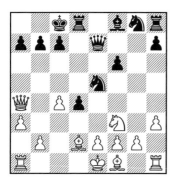

Black mates in 5:

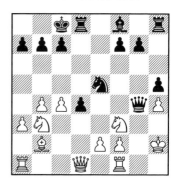

Black to move:

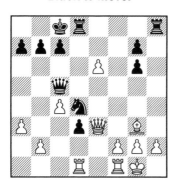

Black to move:

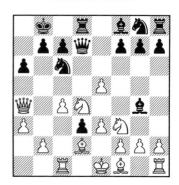

Black to move:

Black to move:

Black to move:

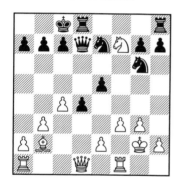

Black to move:

Black to move:

Black to move:

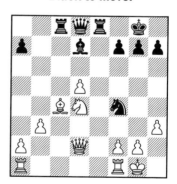

Black to move:

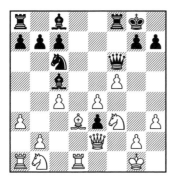

Black to move:

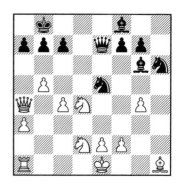

Black to move:

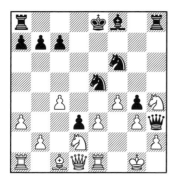

Black to move:

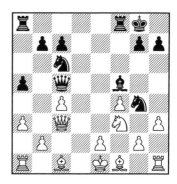

Black to move:

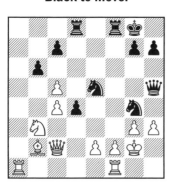

Black mates in 7:

White mates in three:

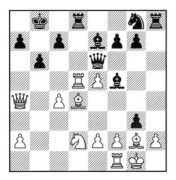

White to move:

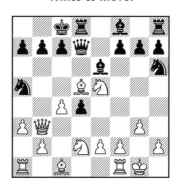

White mates in four:

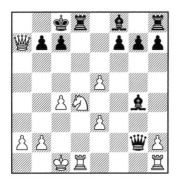

White to move:

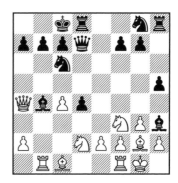

White to move:

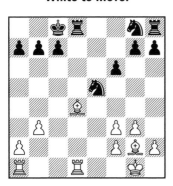

White to move:

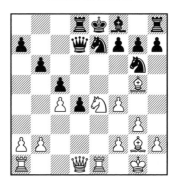

White to move:

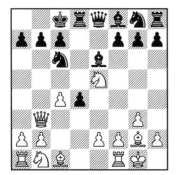

White to move:

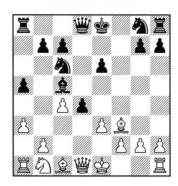

White to move:

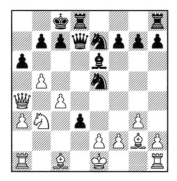

White to move:

Chapter 12

The Winawer Countergambit (D10)

This opening can proceed in a number of ways. Note that the first two main variations involve a recapture of the e5-pawn by the black queen. Thus Black, who concedes the first move, then moves the queen twice. Considering that 3 tempi = 1 pawn, the Winawer may be called a "true" gambit.

Here are the two most popular continuations yielding an open position. White still needs to develop, and Black must protect the advanced pawn without sacrificing tempi.

1. d4 d5 2. c4 c6 3. ♘c3 e5 4. dxe5 d4 5. ♘e4 ♕a5+ 6. ♗d2 ♕xe5 7. ♘g3:

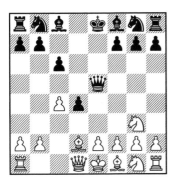

Or –
1. d4 d5 2. c4 c6 3. ♘c3 e5 4. cxd5 cxd5 5. dxe5 d4 6. ♘e4 ♕a5+:

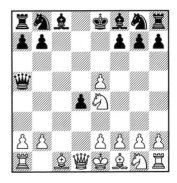

In the closed variation, Black needs to protect the pawn chain, while White develops along more natural lines. It's an Advance French with an extra move for the "French" side.

1. d4 d5 2. c4 c6 3. ♘c3 e5 4. e3 e4:

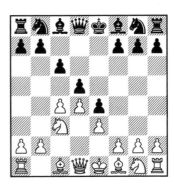

Our first example is an intricate queen trap. Every White piece save the h1-rook participates.

83

Andrew Ho – Frisco Del Rosario
Concord 1995

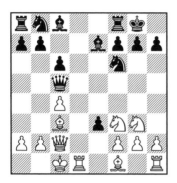

13. b4 ♕b6 14. c5 1-0 (14...♕c7 15. ♗e5)

In the following position, it is White's queen which is driven to the fatal square.

Justo García Suárez – José María Suárez Arboleya, Asturias 1997

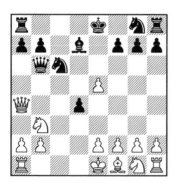

11...♘b4 12. ♕a5 ♕xa5 13. ♘xa5 ♘c2+ 14. ♔d2 ♘xa1 15. ♘xb7 ♖b8 16. ♘d6+ ♔e7 17. ♔c1 f6 18. exf6+ ♘xf6 19. ♘c4 ♖hc8 20. b3 ♘e4 0-1

White has not managed to complete development, and the game ends quickly.

William Bennet – Jonny Hector
St. Hélier 2005

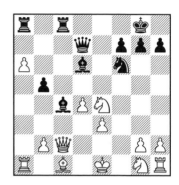

21...♘xe4 22. ♕xe4 ♗d5 0-1

The game below is from our third variation, though in this case we have a half-closed position, as both e-pawns captured on d4. White has developed faster and has a series of forcing moves.

Mikhail Simantsev – Sergey Sukharev
Kharkov 2009

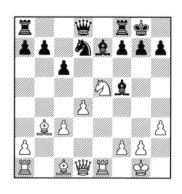

15. ♘xf7 ♖xf7 16. ♗xf7+ ♔xf7 17. ♕f3 ♔g6 18. g4 ♗c2 19. ♖e2 1-0

In this example, Black's queen ignores her attacker and White has to give up his own queen to avoid mate.

Richard Neitzsch – Ludwig Stenz
Biel 2001

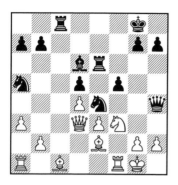

21...♗xh2+ 22. ♘xh2 ♖h6 23. ♕xe4 fxe4 24. ♖f4 ♕xh2+ 25. ♔f2 ♘b3 26. ♗g4 ♕h4+ 27. ♔e2 ♘xa1 28. ♗xc8 ♕g3 29. ♗d2 ♕xg2+ 30. ♖f2 ♕g6 31. ♗b4 ♕a6+ 32. ♔d1 ♖h1+ 0-1

While at 28 moves it is not a miniature, the following game is inspired. Black has two extra pieces and the only move that wins for White is a further sacrifice, this time of the exchange. Clearly there is a lot of give-and-take in this countergambit.

Marc Becker – Guido Gössling
Germany 1996

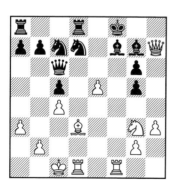

28. ♖xf7+ (28. ♘h5 gxh5 29. ♖xf7+ works, too) 28...♔xf7 29. ♖f1+ ♔e6 30. ♕xg6+ (30. ♕xg7 ♘e8 31. ♕xg6+ ♘ef6 32. ♗f5+ ♔xe5 33. ♗xd7 ♖xd7 34. ♕xg5+ ♔d6 35. ♖xf6+) ♗f6 31. exf6:

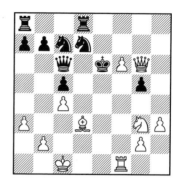

31...♖g8 (31...♘e8 32. f7+ ♘ef6 33. ♗f5+ ♔d6 34. ♗xd7 ♕xd7 35. ♖d1+) 32. ♕f5+ ♔f7 33. ♕h7+ 1-0

Puzzles

Now for some supplementary puzzles from Winawer miniatures. (Solutions on p. 142.)

White mates in three:

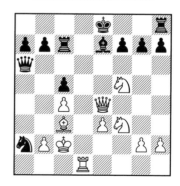

Black mates in 5:

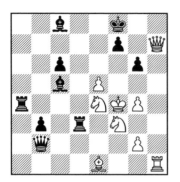

Black to move:

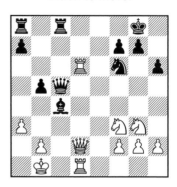

Black to move:

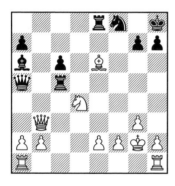

Black to move:

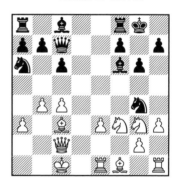

White to move:

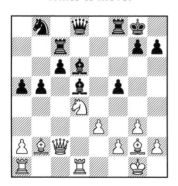

White to move:

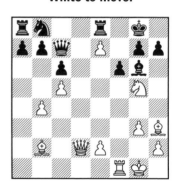

White to move:

White to move:

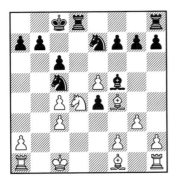

White to move:

White to move:

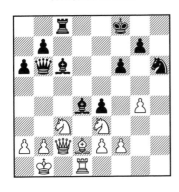

Black to move:

White to move:

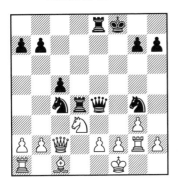

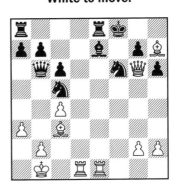

Chapter 13

The Geller Gambit (D15)

T his variation of the Slav De-fense begins with White giving away the c4-pawn. In return he develops a strong center and soon pushes a pawn to e5. Black can hold the pawn on c4 with the b-pawn, but this creates targets and outposts for White. It's an unbalanced game rich with pins, forks, sacrifices, and hang-ing pieces.

1. d4 d5 2. c4 c6 3. ♘c3 ♘f6 4. ♘f3 dxc4 5. e4:

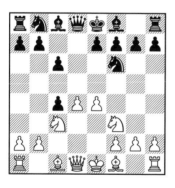

Here is a typical position. White is focused on the center. Black has space, but it's not clear what his targets are. White uses his strong central position to invade at d6 with the king's knight, making way for the f3-bishop to hit the rook at a8.

**Luc Winants – Jacob Murey
Haringey 1988**

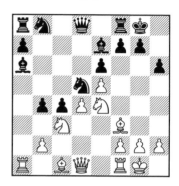

14. ♘xd5 exd5 15. ♘d6 ♗xd6 16. ♗xd5 ♗c7 17. ♗xa8 ♗b6 18. d5 c3 19. ♖e1 ♕h4 20. ♗e3 cxb2 21. ♖b1 ♘d7 22. ♗xb6 ♖xa8 23. ♗d4 ♗b7 24. e6 fxe6 25. dxe6 ♘c5 26. e7 ♖e8 27. f3 ♘a4 28. ♗f2 1-0

The following game features an interesting sacrifice, which illus-trates that events on f7 can affect the queenside too.

**Eric Brondum – Steen Petersen
Copenhagen 1993**

13. ♘xf7 ♔xf7 (13...♖g8 14. ♘d6+ ♔d7 15. ♘xb5 ♕b6 16. ♗xc4) 14. ♕f3+ ♔g815. ♕xa8 ♘c6 16. ♗f3 ♗d7 17. 0-0 1-0

Having invested a pawn on e6, White collects interest.

Octav Troianescu – Cedendemberel Lhagvasuren, Ulan Bator 1956

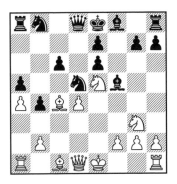

13. ♘xf5 exf5 14. ♕h5+ g6 15. ♘xg6 ♘f6 16. ♘e5+ 1-0

The first player pushes the d-pawn with impunity:

Alexander Schneider – Tamás Utasi Balatonberény 1989

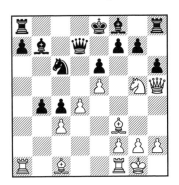

15. d5 ♘xe5 (15...exd5 16. e6; 15... g6 16. dxc6 ♗xc6 17. ♕h4 ♗e7 18. ♖d1 ♗d5 19. ♗xd5 exd5 20. ♕d4 hxg5 21.

e6) 16. dxe6 ♘xf3+ 17. ♘xf3 (better is 17. gxf3 ♕d5 18. ♕xf7+) ♕xe6 18. ♖e1 0-0-0 19. ♖xe6 fxe6 20. ♗f4 b3 21. ♕f7 1-0

In the following game, White simply storms through the enemy pawn ramparts.

Sarhan Guliev – Jurij Markov Vladivostok 1995

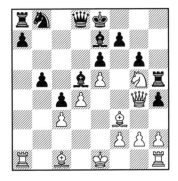

17. ♘xe6 (17...♗xe6 18. ♕e4; 17... fxe6 18. ♕xg6+) 1-0

Here is another look at d6 as an outpost for the knight. This time, however, the idea is to operate in conjunction with the dark-squared bishop.

Alex Dunne – J. Schweinsberg Corr. 1993

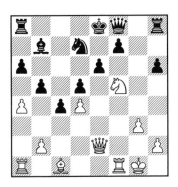

20. ♗f4 e5 (20...♔d8 21. ♘d6 ♗c6 22. ♘xf7+) 21. ♗xe5 (21. dxe5 ♘c5 22. ♘d6+ ♔e7 23. ♗e3) ♘xe5 22. ♕xe5+ ♔d7 23. ♘d6 1-0

A knight on d6 can make a queen sacrifice possible:

Petr Fajman – Ivo Zemánek
Czech Republic 1996

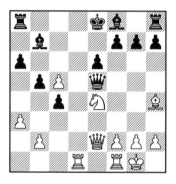

21. ♘d6+ 1-0 (if 21...♗xd6, then 22. cxd6 ♕xe2 23. d7+ mates)

Black has a better reply here, but White's control of the center spells the difference.

Stefano Sala – Michael Walter
Internet 2001

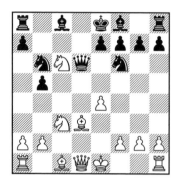

10. e5 ♕xc6 (better is 10...♕e6 11. f4 ♘fd5 12. ♘d4, and if 12...♕d7, then 13. ♗xb5 wins the queen) 11. ♗xb5 ♕xb5 12. ♘xb5 ♘fd5 13. 0-0 f6 14. exf6 ♘xf6 15. ♘c7+ ♔f7 16. ♕b3+ ♔g6 17. ♕g3+ ♔f5 18. ♕g5+ ♔e4 19. ♕e3+ ♔f5 20. ♕g5+ ♔e4 21. ♖e1+ ♔d4 22. ♕e3+ ♔c4 23. ♕c3# 1-0

Puzzles

Now for supplementary puzzles from Geller Gambit miniatures. (Solutions on p. 145.)

White to move:

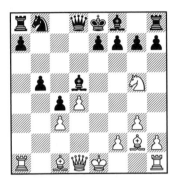

White to move:

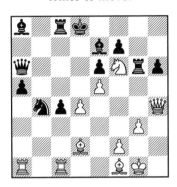

White to move:

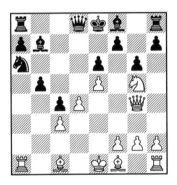

White mates in 6:

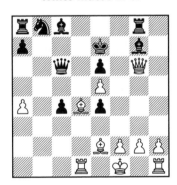

White to move:

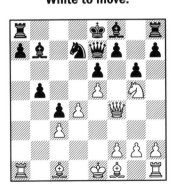

White to move:

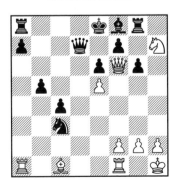

White to move:

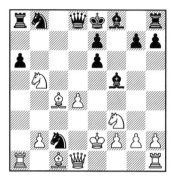

White to move:

White to move:

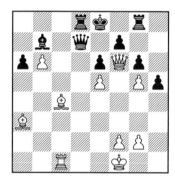

White to move:

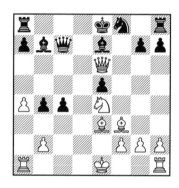

White to move:

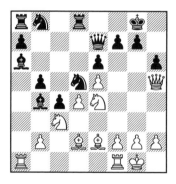

White to move:

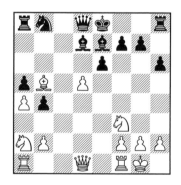

White to move:

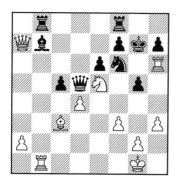

White to move:

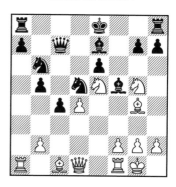

White to move:

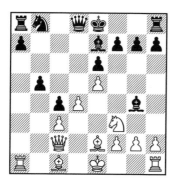

White to move:

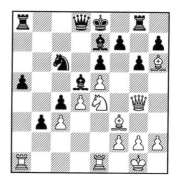

White to move:

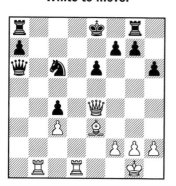

White to move:

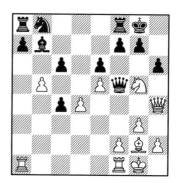

Black mates in four:

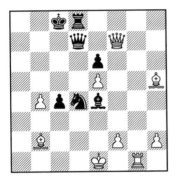

Black to move:

Black to move:

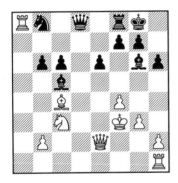

Black to move:

Black to move:

Black to move:

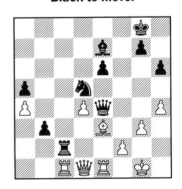

Chapter 14

The Blumenfeld Gambit (E10)

1. d4 ♘f6 2. c4 e6 3. ♘f3 c5 4. d5 b5:

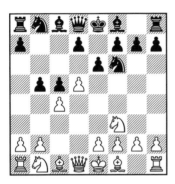

This is the starting point, from which Blumenfeld games split into two major branches with little in the way of transposition:

1. d4 ♘f6 2. c4 e6 3. ♘f3 c5 4. d5 b5 5. ♗g5 exd5 6. cxd5 d6 7. e4 a6 8. a4:

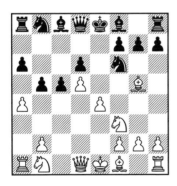

In this line the gambit has been declined, but White's dark-squared bishop exercises a larger scope and pins the knight.

Or –

1. d4 ♘f6 2. c4 e6 3. ♘f3 c5 4. d5 b5 5. dxe6 fxe6 6. cxb5 d5 7. e3 ♗d6:

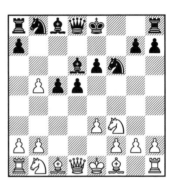

The gambit proper: Black has an imposing pawn front, while White's king will seek safety on his right flank.

The f3-knight may be the best natural target for the gambiteer. Black has the open f-file; the a8-h1 diagonal is easily utilized; and the ...e5-e4 pawn push hangs in the air.

Iulia Gromova – Vera Nebolsina
Sochi 2008

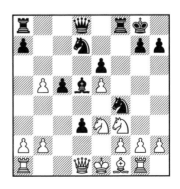

18...♗xf3 19. ♕xf3 (19. gxf3 ♘xe5 20. ♖g3 ♘h5 21. ♖h3 ♘xf3+ 22. ♖xf3 ♕a5+ 23. ♕d2 ♕xd2+ 24. ♔xd2 ♖xf3) ♕a5+ 20. ♔d1 ♕a4+ 21. b3 ♕d4 22. ♖c1 ♘xe5 (22...♘e2) 23. ♕g3 ♕b2 0-1

Now for a more violent approach:

Dan Andersen – Gunnar Finnlaugsson
Copenhagen 2007

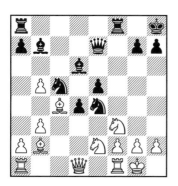

18...♖xf3 19. gxf3 ♘g5 20. ♘xd4 exd4 21. ♗e2 ♕e5 22. ♖e1 ♕xh2+ 23. ♔f1 ♕h1# 0-1

Black is just a move away from yielding a draw by perpetual check, but she decides to crash a rook into f3.

Irina Len – Natalia Zhukova
Kallithea 2008

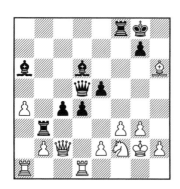

24...♖bxf3 (24...gxh6 25. ♕g6+

draws) 25. exf3 ♕xf3+ 26. ♔g1 d3 27. ♘xd3 cxd3 (27...♗b7 28. ♕xc4+ ♔h8 29. ♘f4 ♖xf4) 28. ♖f1 ♕xf1+ 29. ♖xf1 ♖xf1+ 30. ♔xf1 dxc2+ 0-1

There are sacrifices on f2 as well:

Zdeněk Vorček – Vojtěch Kovář
Říčany 2009

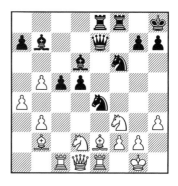

18...♘xf2 19. ♗xf6 (19.♔xf2 ♕e3+ mates) ♕e3 20. ♘c4 ♘xh3+ 0-1

The f-file is not for rooks only. There follows a stunning attack:

Lukáš Černoušek – David Navara
Czech Republic 2009

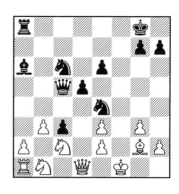

20...♕f8+ 21. ♔g1 ♕f2+ 22. ♔h1 ♗xe2 23. ♕e1 ♗d3 24. ♘xc3 ♗xc2 25. ♕xf2 ♘xf2+ 26. ♔g1 ♘e4 27. ♖c1 ♘b4 28. ♘a4 ♖c8 0-1

In addition, there is an important outpost for the invaders at e4.

Heinz Wirz – Sophie Milliet
Basel 2010

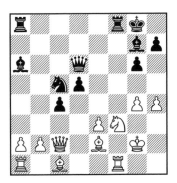

23...♘e4 24. ♗d1 ♕g3+ 25. ♔h1 c3 0-1

What stratagems are there for White to implement in the Blumenfeld? Half-open files come in handy:

Juan Carlos Lobato Gómez – Manuel Castro Molero, Asturias 1986

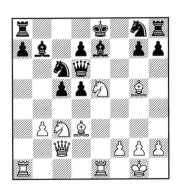

16. ♘b5 ♕b8 17. ♗g6+ ♔d8 (17... hxg6 18. ♕xg6+ ♔d8 19. ♘f7+ ♔c8 20. ♘fd6+) 18. ♘f7+ ♔c8 19. ♘xh8 ♗g5 20. ♖e8+ ♗d8 21. ♘f7 d4 22. ♕xc5 1-0

Next we have a slight variation on the theme.

Aleksandr Veingold – Jari Järvelä
Turku 2001

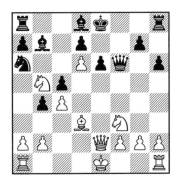

15. ♘e5 ♕g5 (15...♗c6 16. ♕h5+ g6 17. ♗xg6+ ♔f8 18. ♗e4) 16. ♗g6+ ♔f8 17. ♘xd7+ 1-0

The open f-file is also accessible from c4:

C. Barro – G. Arabito
Cecchina 1997

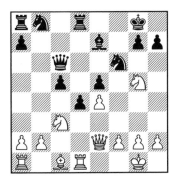

18. ♕c4+ 1-0 (if 18...♔h8, then 19. ♘f7+ mates)

A wayward queen can find herself imprisoned in a coordinated force field of hostile pieces:

Zviad Izoria – Teona Odisharia
Batumi 2003

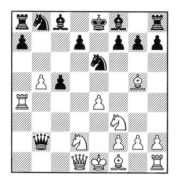

12. ♘c4 ♕c3+ 13. ♗d2 ♕f6 14. e5
♕g6 (14...♕f5 15. ♗e2 g5 16. ♘b6) 15.
♘d6+ ♗xd6 16. ♘h4 ♗xe5 17. ♘xg6
hxg6 18. ♕f3 1-0

Adnan Karahmetović – Hamza Mujić
Tuzla 20067

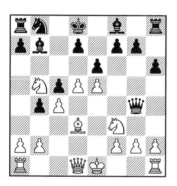

12. h3 ♕xg2 13. ♖h2 ♕xh2 14. ♘xh2
exd5 15. ♕f3 1-0

Here is an example from the 5. ♗g5
Blumenfeld. White creates leverage
with his own pawn phalanx.

Oivind Andersen – Vidar Taksrud
Norway 1997

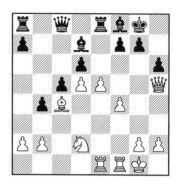

20. e6 fxe6 (or 20...g6 21. ♕g4) 21.
dxe6 ♖xe6 22. f5 1-0

Even the lowly a-pawn can serve as
a decisive weapon.

Sergei Shipov – Alexander Scetinin
Cappelle-la-Grande 1995

15. a6 c4 (15...♗a8 16. a7 ♕d8 17.
♘xd6) 16. ♘xd6 ♕xd6 17. ♗xf6 ♗a8 18.
♗c3 b5 19. ♕d2 ♖f7 20. ♘g5 ♖fe7 21.
♗b4 ♘c5 22. ♘e4 ♘xe4 23. ♗xd6 ♘xd2
24. ♗xd2 1-0

Puzzles

Supplementary puzzles from miniatures. (Solutions on p. 149.)

Black to move:

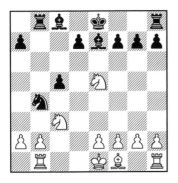

Black to move:

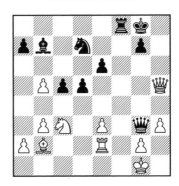

Black to move:

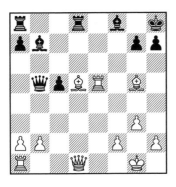

Black to move:

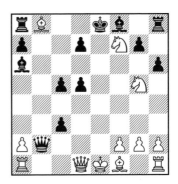

Black to move:

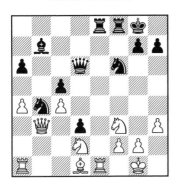

Black to move:

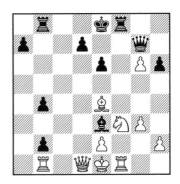

Black to move:

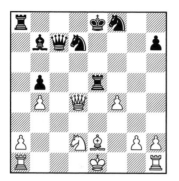

Black to move:

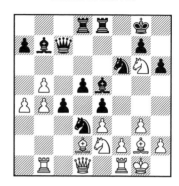

Black to move:

Black to move:

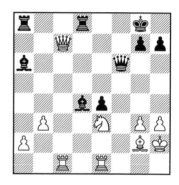

Black to move:

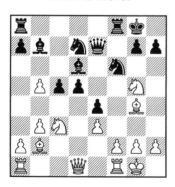

White to move:

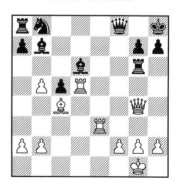

White to move:

White to move:

White mates in 5:

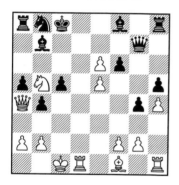

White to move:

White to move:

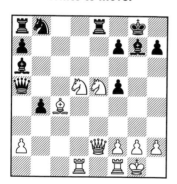

Chapter 15

Queen's Indian Defense – Polugaevsky Variation (E17)

This lively gambit stems from an opening with a stolid reputation, the Queen's Indian Defense:

1. d4 ♘f6 2. c4 e6 3. ♘f3 b6 4. g3 ♗b7 5. ♗g2 ♗e7 6. 0-0 0-0 7. d5 exd5 8. ♘h4:

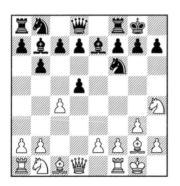

From the starting position, the main variation runs 8...c6 9. cxd5 ♘xd5 10. ♘f5 ♘c7:

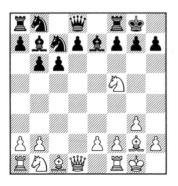

The game now continues with either 11. e4 d5, or 11. ♘c3 d5 12. e4 ♗f6. While the e4- and d5-pawns will shut down the light-squared bishops, these are in no way locked up. Black's position is generally compact, with both knights on the queenside by move 10. White tries to take advantage of this and create weaknesses on Black's castled king before reinforcements can arrive.

In the first example, Black is up two pawns. The simple 15. ♕xh5 ♗f6 leaves White without a strategy, so he plunges a second piece on the horns of a pawn.

Konstantin Kostin – Denis Skrynnikov
Kaluga 2003

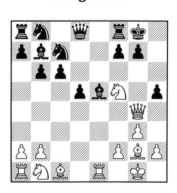

15. ♘h6+ ♔h7 16. ♕xh5 gxh6 (16... g6 17. ♕xe5) 17. ♕xh6+ ♔g8 18. ♖xe5 f5 19. ♕g6+ ♔h8 20. ♗g5 1-0

In this example, Black is better positioned to meet the attack, but White's idea is very similar and soon he is ahead by a pair of pawns.

Andre Lisanti – Temur Parulava
Germany 1995

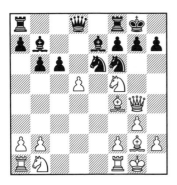

15. ♘h6+ ♔h8 16. ♘xf7+ ♖xf7 17. ♕xe6 ♕g8 18. dxc6 ♗c8 19. ♕b3 ♗a6 20. ♖e1 ♗c5 21. ♘c3 ♕f8 22. ♘e4 ♘xe4 23. ♖xe4 ♖c8 24. ♖ae1 h6 25. h4 ♔h7 26. ♖a4 ♗xf2+ 27. ♔xf2 ♕c5+ 28. ♖e3 ♖d8 29. ♗e4+ ♔h8 30. ♕xf7 ♕b5 31. ♖xa6 ♕xa6 32. ♗d3 ♕c8 1-0

This attack adds the queenside to the battle zone.

Ludwig Bielmeier – Sebastian Völker
Kaufbeuren 1998

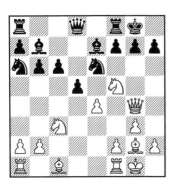

14. exd5 cxd5 15. ♘xd5 ♗xd5 16. ♗xd5

White threatens the rook and the only piece protecting against mate:

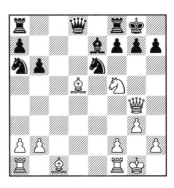

16...♗f6 (16...♖b8 17. ♗xe6) 17. ♘h6+ ♔h8 18. ♘xf7+ ♖xf7 19. ♗xa8 ♘ac5 (19...♕xa8 20. ♕xe6) 20. ♗g2 1-0

In the Queen's Indian, Black aims to create a solid structure, but sometimes that comes at the expense of mobility and flexibility. A small material sacrifice at the right time can crack the doors open.

Alexander Razmyslov – Manuel Peña
Gómez, Coria del Río (Spain) 2003

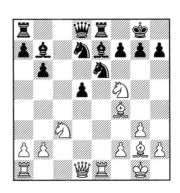

16. ♘xd5 ♗xd5 (16...♗c5 17. ♘c7

♗xg2 [17...♘xc7 18. ♖xe8+ ♘xe8 19. ♗xb7] 18. ♘xe8) 17. ♗xd5:

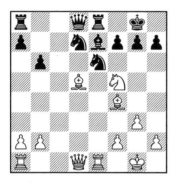

17...♗b4 (17...♖c8 18. ♖xe6 ♘f6 19. ♘xe7+) 18. ♖xe6 ♖xe6 (18...fxe6 19. ♕d4 ♘f6 20. ♗xa8) 19. ♕d4 ♖f6 20. ♗xa8 ♖xf5 21. ♗c6 g5 22. ♗e3 1-0

Both players in the following game are strong masters rated close to 2400. Black is a pawn ahead, but his pieces occupy only three ranks on the board. White invests a knight in the offensive, and the game is soon over.

Maxim Polyakov – Konstantin Borsuk
Donetsk 2007

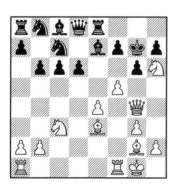

18. ♘xf7 ♔xf7 (18...♕d7 19. ♗d4+ ♔f8 20. ♘g5 ♗xg5 21. fxg6+) 19. fxg6+ ♔g8 20. ♕h5 1-0

White's army enjoys great mobility in the Polugaevsky. Here White attacks the queenside at the same time he threatens mate on the opposite wing.

Henrik Molvig – Nicolai Getz
Copenhagen 2007

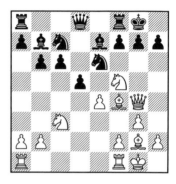

15. ♗xc7 ♕xc7 16. exd5 cxd5 17. ♘xd5 ♗xd5 18. ♗xd5 ♗c5 (18...♖ac8 19. ♗xe6) 19. ♗xa8 ♖xa8 20. b4 ♗e7 21. ♘h6+ ♔h8 22. ♕f3 1-0

Below we witness one of the most sudden queen traps ever to take place. One quiet move and Her Majesty is doomed.

Dragan Barlov – Marcos Adrián Pérez
Felipe, El Sauzal (Spain) 2006

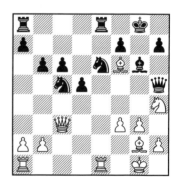

28. ♕d2 d4 29. ♖e5 1-0

Puzzles

Now for some supplementary puzzles from Polugaevsky Variation miniatures.
(Solutions on p. 152.)

White mates in three:

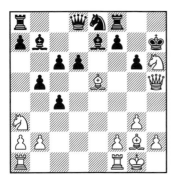

White to move:

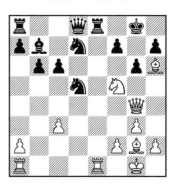

White to move:

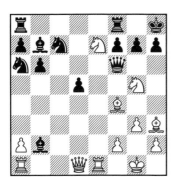

White to move:

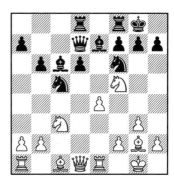

White to move:

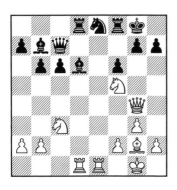

White to move:

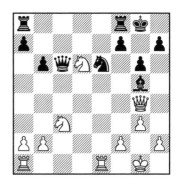

White to move:

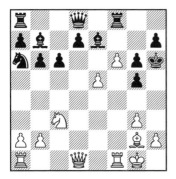

White to move:

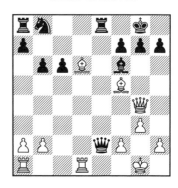

White to move:

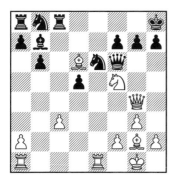

White to move:

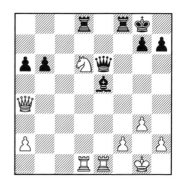

White to move:

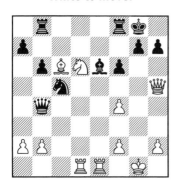

White to move:

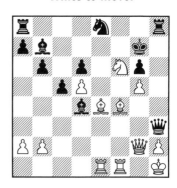

White to move:

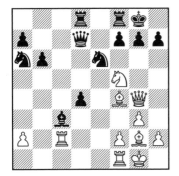

White to move:

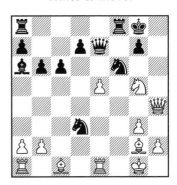

White to move:

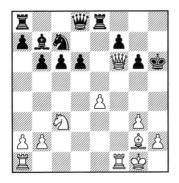

Black to move:

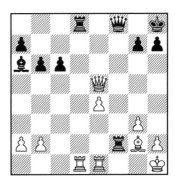

Solutions

Chapter 1: The Lisitsin Gambit

Dieter Daum – Egon Betz
Bad Wiessee 2002

White to move:

8. ♕h5+ g6 (8...♔e7 9. ♕e5+ ♔f7 10. ♗c4+ ♔g6 11. ♕xe4+ leads to mate) 9. ♕e5+ ♕e7 10. ♕xh8 d5 (10...♕b4+ 11. ♗d2 ♘xd2 12. ♘xd2 ♕xb2 13. ♖b1 ♕xc2 14. ♖b3) 11. ♗d3 ♗f5 12. ♕e5 ♕xe5 13. dxe5 c5 14. f3 1-0

Holger Göttmann – Andreas Sauter
Bingen 1996

White to move:

17. g5 ♗e7 18. ♗xh7+ 1-0

Christopher Overbeck – Alena Kuhn
Dortmund 2003

White to move:

14. ♘xe7+ ♕xe7 15. ♘d5 ♘xd5 (15... ♗xd5 16. exd5 b6 17. ♗xa5 bxa5 18. ♗a6+ mates) 16. exd5 ♗xd5 17. ♗xa5 ♗xg2 18. ♕g4+ ♔b8 19. ♕xg2 1-0

Michael Rohde – Semyon Palatnik
Philadelphia 1990

White to move:

19. ♗f7+ 1-0 (19...♔f8 20. ♗g6+ ♔g8 21. ♕d5+; 19...♔d7 20. ♕g4#; 19...♕xf7 20. ♖xf7 ♔xf7 21. ♕f3+)

Alexander Matthaei – Klaus Ropers
Münster 1993

White to move:

24. ♗xh6 1-0

Christian Bauer – Krzysztof Pytel
Reims 1994

White to move:

14. ♗c4+ d5 15. ♗xd5+ ♔h8 (15...
♘xd5 16. ♕xh7#) 16. ♘xh7 ♗g4+ 17.
f3 ♗xf3+ 18. gxf3 g5 19. ♘xf8+ gxh4
20. ♘g6+ 1-0

Richard Forster – M. Mahamuti
Bern 1996

White to move:

23. ♖f3 ♖f6 (23...♘f6 24. ♗xc5 bxc5
25. ♖h3 ♘h5 26. ♕g4; 23...♕f6 24.
♕h3) 24. ♗xc5 bxc5 25. ♖h3 1-0

Csaba Kerék – Simon Nándor
Miskolc 1997

White to move:

13. ♗xb5 1-0 (on 13...♗b7 or 13...
cxb5, White replies 14. ♘d5)

Peter Larsen – Jes West Knudsen
Greve 1999

White to move:

15. ♘xh7+ ♔f7 16. ♕h5+ g6 17.
♕xd5+ 1-0 (17...♗e6 18. ♕xb7+)

Jorge Szmetan – Daniel Barría
Santiago de Chile 1999

White to move:

14. ♗d3 ♕f6 15. ♘xh7 ♕xe5 (better but still losing is 15...♕f7 16. ♗g5 ♘d5 17. ♗xe7 ♘xe7 18. ♘g5 ♕f6 19. ♖de1) 16.♗g6# 1-0

Jovan Geleta – Andor Borsos
Senta 2002

White to move:

15. ♗g8 ♖h8 (15...♖g7 16. ♗xh6) 16. ♘f6+ exf6 17. ♕f7# 1-0

Pavel Rakus – Vladan Pecha
Ostrava 2005

White to move:

21. ♘xd7 ♗xh2 (21...♔xd7 22. ♗xf5+) 22. ♘b5+ ♔xd7 23. ♗xf5+ ♘e6 (23...♔c6 24.♕f3+) 24. ♖xe6 1-0

Csaba Sigér – Simon Nándor
Hungary 1997

Black to move

21...♘xd3 22. ♖xe6 (22. ♔xd3 ♘c5+) ♖xe6 23. ♔xd3 ♖d8+ 0-1

Jon D. Reese – D. Boyes
Leeds 2001

Black to move:

18...♖xc3+ 19. ♔d2 (19. bxc3 ♗xa3+ 20. ♔d2 ♘xb5) ♖xa3 20. ♗f6 (20. bxa3 ♘xb5 21. ♗f6 ♗h6+ 22. ♔e1 ♖f8) ♗b4+ 21. ♔c1 ♘b3+ 0-1

Karl Robatsch – Bent Larsen
Moscow 1956

Black to move:

17...♘xe3 18. fxe3 ♕c3+ 19. ♔f2 ♗c5 0-1 (20. ♕xd5+ ♔e7)

Katalin Décsey – Júlia Horváth
Lillafüred 1999

Black to move:

15...♖xf1+ 16. ♔xf1 ♕xh2 17. ♕e2 ♖f8+ 18. ♔e1 ♕g1+ 19. ♔d2 ♖f2 0-1

Bella Airijan – Anastasya Antipova
Nizhny Novgorod 1999

Black to move:

20...♖xf3 21. gxf3 ♕h5 22. ♘f4 ♕h4 23. ♖g1 ♗xf4 0-1

Chapter 2: Scandinavian Defense – Portuguese Gambit

Vladimir Dimitrov – Kevin Spraggett
Úbeda 1996

Black to move:

20...♖xd4 0-1 (21. ♕xd4 ♖d8)

Leonid Tkach – Graham Free
New York 1998

Black mates in 5:

20...♖e2+ 0-1

Tim Pernes – Xiaodong Yu
Dallas 2000

Black to move:

20...♖xe2 21. ♖xe2 ♖xe2 22. ♕xe2 ♕xd4+ 23. ♔f1 ♕xa1+ 24. ♔f2 ♕d4+ 0-1

Alexandre Santos – José Fernando Cubas, São Paulo 2002

Black to move:

18...♗g5+ 19. ♔c2 ♗d3+ 20. ♔b2 ♖xe1 21. ♗xg5 ♖xa1 22. ♔xa1 ♗f1 0-1

Merijn van Delft – Dolf Meijer Leiden 1997

Black to move:

18...♖g2+ 19. ♔xg2 ♕xe2+ 20. ♔h3 ♕xf3+ 21. ♔h4 ♖g8 0-1

Sergiy Zavgorodniy – Alexander Zubarev, Alushta 2001

Black mates in three:

23...♕f5 0-1

Timothy J. Upton – Andrew D. Martin Isle of Lewis 1995

Black to move:

20...♖xd4 21. ♖xd4 ♖xd4 22. ♖xd4 (22. ♘xg6 ♖xd1+ 23. ♕f1 f3) ♕b1+ 0-1

Sauli Keskinen – Olli Salmensuu Helsinki 1998

Black mates in three:

28...♕h1+ (Δ 29...♗xg3+) 0-1

Arnaud Fournet – Thierry Gouret France 2000

Black to move:

11...♘xc3 12. bxc3 ♕xd3 13. ♗xd3 ♗xc3+ 14. ♔e2 ♗xa1 15. ♖xa1 0-0 16. ♖b1 b6 17. ♗b5 ♖ac8 18. h3 ♗f5 19. ♗a4

♖fd8 20. ♖b2 ♗e4 21. c3 ♘a5 0-1

Giorgi Sulashvili – Matthieu Cornette
Gurzuf 2000

Black mates in four:

15...♘xa2+ 16. ♔xa2 ♕f5 0-1

Vladislav Nevednichy – Zdravko
Vuković, Nikšić 2000

Black to move:

24...♘b4 25. ♗e4 (25. ♗xh7 f6) f5
26. ♗f3 ♘c2+ 27. ♔f1 ♘xa1 28. ♔g2
♗c6 29. ♗xc6 ♖xd2+ 30. ♔h3 ♖e6 0-1

I. Gontcharova – Tatjana Kostjuk
Orsk 2000

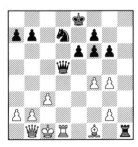

Black to move:
26...♕xd1+ 0-1

Martin Schneider – Sergei Krivoshey
Aschach 2001

Black to move:

15...♖xb2 16. ♕xd8 (16. ♕a4 ♖b4 17.
♕a3 ♖d4+ 18. ♗d2 ♗f4) ♗c2+ (mates)
0-1

Robert Fiala – Petr Císler
Czech Republic 2001

Black to move:

15...♗c5+ 16. ♔e2 (16. ♔e1 ♗b4+
17. ♕xb4 ♕c1+ 18. ♔f2 ♘xb4 19. ♗b5+
♔c8 20. a3 ♘c2) ♖e8+ 17. ♔d1 ♗b4
and mates 0-1

Fernando J. M. Costa – Paulo Dias
Portugal 2001

Black mates in two:

30...♗b4+ 0-1

Mehdi Hasan – Hilton Bennett
Kuala Lumpur 2006

Black mates in two:

21...♛xh2+ 0-1

Enrique Garzón – Alexis Ferrara
Buenos Aires 2004

Black to move:

16...♛f5 17. ♔g2 ♗xc5 18. ♗xc5 ♖xd5 19. ♛e2 ♖xc5 20. ♘c3 ♖e8 21. ♛e3 g6 22. ♘e2 ♛xh3+ 23. ♔xh3 ♖h5+ 24. ♔g4 ♘h2+ 0-1

Olivia Smith – Tim Kett
Hensol Park 2006

Black to move:

25...♘e5 26. ♛e2 (26. ♖b3 ♛d6 27. ♖d1 ♖xc4; 26. ♛f2 ♖xd4) ♘d3 27. ♖xb6 ♘xc1 28. ♛e5 ♖xd4 29. ♖xg6 0-1

Herbert Schmid – Volker Scheeff
Bad Homburg 2007

Black to move:

17...♘b4 18. ♖c1 ♘d3+ 0-1

Sergey Daryev – Lyudmila Petrova
Odessa 2007

Black to move:

21...♖d1+ 22. ♔f2 ♖f1+ 23. ♔g3 ♗xf4+ 24. ♔g4 ♗xe3 25. ♗xe3 ♖xa1 0-1

Christopher Briscoe – Ankush
Khandelwal, Uxbridge 2009

Black to move:

14...♗xg3 15. fxg3 d3 16. ♗xd3 ♖xd3 17. ♕e2 ♖hd8 18. ♘e4 ♘d419. ♕xd3 ♘xf3+ 20. ♖xf3 ♖xd3 21 . ♖af1 ♕h2# 0-1

Vasiliy Tugarin – Alexander Badmatsyrenov, Irkutsk 2009

Black to move:

18...♖xg5 19. d5 ♗h6 20. ♔h1 ♘b4 21. ♕xe7 ♕d6 22. ♕xd6 cxd6 23. ♘d4 ♖xg2 24. f4 ♖b2 25. ♖f3 ♖gg2 26. h3 ♖gf2 27. ♖e3 ♗xf4 28. ♖e4 ♘d3 29. ♖e7 ♘e5 30. ♖e1 ♗e3 0-1

Piotr Dukaczewski – Martínez Laguna 1996

White to move:

20. ♘xc6 bxc6 (20...♕c7 21. ♘xd8) 21. ♕a6+ ♔b8 22. ♕xc6 ♘d5 23. ♗xd5 ♖xd5 24. ♖xd5 1-0

Gulnara Zhumanbekova – Natalya Grebenschikova, Neftekamsk 2000

White to move:

21. ♖d6 ♕e7 22. ♕d4 ♘f6 23. ♖xf6 1-0

Javier García Ramos – Vicente Ramón Andrés Julia, Mislata (Spain) 2004

White mates in 5:

18. ♘d6+ cxd6 19. ♕c6+ ♔b8 20. ♗xa6 1-0

Oliver Cooley – Nigel Povah England 2008

White to move:

16. ♗g5 ♖xd4 17. ♕b3 ♖xd1 18. ♖xd1 ♘d4 19. ♗xh4 fxe4 20. ♖xd4 ♗c5 21 . ♕xe6 + ♔b8 22. ♕xe4 1-0

Douglas Sailer – Kris Verhasselt
Leuven 2006

White to move:

18. ♘e5 ♖de7 (on 18...♘xe5, 19. ♕xa7+ mates) 19. g4 1-0 (19...♕xh3 20. ♘xc6+ mates)

Damien André – Guido De Bouver
Belgium 2005

White to move:

23. ♕xb6 ♖xb6 24. ♘f4+ 1-0

Leonardo Duarte – Lucas Liascovich
Villa Martelli 2004

White mates in 5:

19. ♗h6 ♘h5 20. ♖g8+ 1-0

Guy West – Jérôme Lachaux
Queenstown 2006

White to move:

13. ♕e6 ♘b6 (13...♗f7 14. ♕c6+) 14. f5 ♕xd4 15. ♗e3 1-0

Tomás Serra Olives – Antonio
Ballester Cladera
Palma de Mallorca 2008

White to move:

18. ♗f4 ♔f8 19. ♖xe7 1-0

Thomas Therkildsen – Wilfried
Dehesdin, Le Touquet 2009

White to move:

16. a3 ♕xd1 17. ♖xd1 ♘c2 18. ♖a2 ♘e4 19. f3 ♘d6 20. b3 1-0

Chapter 3: Caro-Kann
Fantasy Variation

László Bárczay – László Vadász
Budapest 1980

White to move:

15. ♘xb5 ♕xd2+ 16. ♔xd2 cxb5 17. ♗d5 ♘a6 1-0

Roland Ekström – T. Winckelmann
Bern 1987

White to move:

17. ♗xa5, and if 17...♕xa5 then 18. ♘xe6+ mates.

Siegfried Heil – Hermann Schmid
Germany 1999

White to move:

12. ♕f3 1-0 (12...♕e7 13. ♕b3+)

Xavier Lebrun – René Koum
Elancourt 2006

White to move:

8. ♘xd4 ♗xd1 9. ♗xf7+ ♔e7 10. ♗xg8 exd4 11. ♗g5+ ♔e8 12. ♗f7+ ♔d7 13. ♖xd1 1-0

Nickolai Peregudov – Vladimir Savon
St. Petersburg 1994

Black mates in four:

19...♗e3+ 20 ♕xe3 ♕d1+ 0-1

Arjun Panchapagesan – E. Palmer
Guernsey 1990

White to move:

15. c4 1-0 (15...♕a5 16. ♘xc6+ bxc6 17. ♕xa5+)

117

Rogvi Nielsen – Martin Noer
Helsingor 2008

Black to move:

15...♖xc3 0-1 (16. bxc3 ♗a3#)

Kristian Trygstad – Gokhan
Gaygusuzoğlu, Kemer (Turkey) 2007

White to move:

12. ♕d4 ♗g6 13. e6 ♕e7 14. ♕xg7
♕xe6+ 15. ♔f2 ♘d7 16. ♖e1 ♗e4 17.
♗d3 ♘gf6 18. ♘c5 1-0

John Bryant – Melikset Khachiyan
Los Angeles 2007

Black to move:

17...♖xa3 18. ♘f3 (18. ♖xa3 ♕c1+
mates; 18. ♕xa3 ♕d2#) ♖xa1+ 0-1

Chapter 4: The Wing Gambit

Henry Bird – NN
London 1895

White mates in two:

12. ♘xg7+ ♗xg7 13. f5# 1-0

Wilfried Pundt – Gerhard Völpel
Niedersachsen 1999

White mates in two:

17. ♕h6+ 1-0

Juan García – Ignacio Rodríguez
Asturias 2000

White mates in two:

15. ♖xh7+ 1-0

Vita Chulivska – Natacha Benmesbah
Heraklio 200

White to move:

17. ♖d4 1-0

Andrew Thomas – Donald Leslie
Chester 1952

Black to move:

14...♕h4 15. ♘e2 g5 16. ♖g1 gxf4 0-1

R. Bass – C. Weberg
Corr. 1962

White to move:

17. ♕d5 ♔c7 18. ♘e6+ ♔b6 19. ♕b3+ (with mate) 1-0

Uwe Kaden – Manfred Büchle
Ruhrgebiet 1996

White to move:

12. ♘c4 1-0 (12...♘xa1 13. ♘xb6 axb6; 12...♕b5 13. ♘d6+ ♗xd6)

Friedel Drewitz – Marianne Krämer
Bad Wörishofen 1996

White to move:

12. ♘xf6+ gxf6 13. ♗xh6 ♖e8 14. ♗xe6 fxe6 15. ♘h4 1-0

Mueller – Lev Aronin
Riga 1968

White to move:

16. ♗d4 ♕c6 17. ♖ac1 ♘b6 18. ♕b3 ♕d7 19. ♘e5 1-0

Branko Panić – Alexander Maier
Deizisau 2003

White to move:

16. ♘xf6 gxf6 17. ♕h5 1-0

James Branson – Jean Gilles de la
Londe, Montigny-le-Bretonneux 2004

White to move:

15. ♘c7+ 1-0 (15...♕xc7 16.♕xf7+ ♔d8 17.♕xf8+ ♗e8 18.♘e6+)

H. Lefevre – Jeremy Silman
U.S. Amateur Team Chp. 1990

Black mates in 7:

18...♗d3+ 0-1 (19. ♕e2 ♖xe2 20. f3 ♖e4+ 21. ♘e2 ♖xe2 22. ♔g1 ♗c5+ 23. bxc5 ♕xc5+ 24. ♔f1 ♕f2#)

Olivier Lequeux – Guillaume Chanoine
Issy-les-Moulineaux 2001

Black to move:

9...♕d4 10. ♘xg4 (10. ♘xc6 ♕e4+ mates) 10... ♕xa1 11. ♕xa1 ♘c2+ 12. ♔d1 ♘xa1 13. ♗e2 ♘b3 14. ♗b2 f6 15. ♘c3 e6 16. ♘b5 ♔f7 17. ♔c2 ♘ba5 18. d4 a6 19. ♘c7 ♖c8 20. ♘xe6 ♘b4+ 0-1

Jean Lamothe – Norman Zalm
Dubai 1986

Black mates in 6:

18...♗xe3+ 19. ♖f2 gxf2+ (19...♖h1+ 20. ♔xh1 ♕h4+ 21. ♔g1 ♗xf2+ 22. ♕xf2 gxf2+ 23. ♔f1 fxe1♕#) 20. ♔f1 ♖h1+ 0-1

Chapter 5: Grand Prix Attack – Tal Gambit

Ilan Kreitner – Paul Ascolese
Mineola (New York) 1993

White mates in four:

24. ♘h6+ 1-0 (24...♔f8 25. ♗xg7+ ♔xg7 26. ♕g4+ ♔f6 27. ♕g5#)

Radek Londýn – Aleš Jedlička
Czech Republic 2004

White mates in 5:

24. ♕xf7+ 1-0 (24...♔xf7 25. ♖e7+ ♔g8 26. f7+ ♖xf7 27. ♖e8+ ♖f8 28. ♖fxf8#)

Rune Djurhuus – Øystein Dannevig
Gausdal 1999

White to move:

25. c5 ♗e5 26. ♗g5 (26. ♕c4+ ♔h8 27. ♗g5) 1-0 (26...♕xg5 27. ♕c4+)

Sopiko Guramishvili – Varvara Repina
Oropesa del Mar 2001

White to move:

17. ♗xf6 gxf6 18. ♕g4+ ♗g5 19. h4 h5 20. ♕xh5 ♗xe3+ 21. dxe3 ♕g3 22. ♘xg3 1-0

Mark Schenker – Ildiko Madl
Zürich 1987

Black to move:

19...♕xg3 20. hxg3 ♗d7 21. ♘g4 ♖xe2 22. ♘xh6+ gxh6 0-1

Jean Nelis – Mladen Palac
Cannes 1990

Black mates in 6:

22...♕d4+ 0-1 (23. ♔h1 ♘f2+ 24. ♔g1 ♘h3+ 25. ♔h1 ♕g1+ 26. ♖xg1 ♘f2#)

Juan García Castro – Francis Maynard
Costa Rica 1998

Black to move:

19...♗g3 20. ♖g1 ♖f2 (intending ...♕xh3) 0-1

Mu Yuchen – David Raheb
Winnipeg 2002

Black to move:

16...♖xd2 17. ♕a4 ♖xb2+ 0-1

Danil Kuzuev – Dmitry Batsanin
Moscow 1997

Black mates in four:

27...♖e3+ 27. ♘f3 ♖xf3+ 28. ♔h4 (28.♔xf3 ♖e3#) ♗d8+ 29. ♔h5 g6# 0-1

Eugene Yanayt – Matthew Bengtson
Framingham (Massachusetts) 2001

Black mates in four:

25...h5+ 0-1

Chapter 6: French Defense – Milner-Barry Attack

Heinrich Gutheil – Thomas Lemańczyk
Germany 1996

Black mates in two:

18...♛g1+ 0-1

Liem Le Quang – Nguyen Nhat Duong
Dong Thap 2000

White mates in three:

16. ♗g6+ (or 16. ♕g6+) 1-0

Béla Molnár – Ralf Junge
Kecskemét 1991

Black mates in three:

23...♛xg2+ 0-1

J.M. Martí Gutiérrez – Jordi García Busquets, Barcelona 2001

White to move:

20. ♖xe6 fxe6 (20...♖d6 21. ♖xd6 ♗xd6 22. ♖e1 ♕d7 23. ♕h4) 21. ♕xe6+ ♖f7 22. ♕e5 1-0

Pavel Novák – Jan Dvořák
Plzeň 2003

White to move:

16. ♘e4 ♕xe5 (if 16...♕b6 17.♘d6+) 17. ♗f4 ♕a5 18. ♘d6+ ♔d8 19. ♘xb7+ 1-0

Oscar Sáez Gabikagogeaskoa – J. Salvador, Palma de Mallorca 1993

White to move:

14. ♗f4 ♛c6 15. ♘c7+ ♔d8 16. ♖c1 ♘f6 17. ♘xa8 b5 18. ♗xe6 ♛xa8 19. ♗xf7 ♛b7 20. ♗c7+ 1-0

17. ♘xf5 1-0 (17...♘xf5 18. ♗xf5 exf5 19. e6 ♛xf4 20. exf7+ ♔d8 21. ♛e7+ ♔c8 22. f8♛+)

Gerhard Brückner – Hilfried Gnauk
Pinneberg 1991

White to move:

18. ♖xe6 (18...♛xe6 19. ♖b7+) 1-0

Alfred Philippi – Patrick Jaspers
Fischbach 1993

White to move:

19. ♘xh4 ♗xh4 20. ♛h5 1-0

Jonas de Vargas Ferreira – Santos
Edson Bastos, Santos (Brazil) 2008

White to move:

18. ♗xe7 ♔xe7 (18...♘xe7 19. ♘c7+)
19. ♛xd5 ♖d8 20. ♛g5+ ♔f8 21. ♘c7 1-0

Mattias Hedlin – Stanislav Midjich
Hallstahammar 1995

White to move:

19. ♗xg6 1-0

Michael Negele – Andreas Morsch
Leverkusen 2001

White to move:

Miklós Szava – Zsolt Szilágyi
Hajdúböszörmény 1996

White to move:

15. ♘b5 ♗c6 16. ♘d6+ ♔d7 17. ♘xf7 ♕e8 18. ♘xh8 hxg5 19. b5 1-0

Raphael Delivre – Bertrand Sainet
Gonfreville 2000

White to move:

14. ♕d3 ♘b8 (14...g6 15. ♖fb1) 15. ♕h7# 1-0

Jesús Carrasco Rodríguez – Francisco Romero, Sants (Spain) 2001

White mates in 5:

13. ♕h5+ g6 14. ♗xg6+ ♔f8 15. ♗h6+ ♘xh6 16. ♕xh6+ ♔g8 17. ♗f7# 1-0

Martin Schneider – Hermann Tomitz
Latschach 2001

White mates in 5:

19. ♗xh7+ ♔xh7 (19... ♔h8 20. ♖g3 g6 21. ♕f6+ ♔xh7 22. ♖h3+ ♔g8 23. ♕h8#) 20. ♖g3 g6 21. ♖h3+ ♔g8 22. ♕f6 ♘xa2 23. ♕h8# 1-0

Marek Cieśla – Bartosz Furman
Rowy 2002

White to move:

17. ♘xd5 1-0

Douglas Lindberg – Alex Viniarski
Churchill 2000

White mates in four:

17. ♕h5+ g6 18. ♗xg6+ ♘xg6 19. ♕xg6+ ♔e7 20. ♗c5# 1-0

Miša Pap – Nikolai Pushkov
Belgrade 2006

White to move:

22. ♗d6 1-0 (22...♖xd6 23. exd6 ♕xd6 24. ♕xh8)

Henri Lavergne – Isabelle Bresard
France 2004

White to move:

18. f6 ♗xe3 19. fxg7 1-0 (19...♗xf2 20. gxh8♕+ ♔e7 21. ♕f6+ ♔f8 22. ♕xf2)

Hagen Poetsch – Klaus Fuchs
Frankfurt 2006

White to move:

13. ♗f4 1-0 (Δ 14. ♘c7+)

Ljilja Drljević – Ana Benderać
Herceg Novi 2005

Black to move:

17....♗b5+ 18. ♔g1 (if 18. ♔e1 ♘d3+) 18...♖d8 0-1

Werner Kugelmann – Thomas Geyer
Germany 1999

Black to move:

22...♖e6 0-1 (23. ♕xd5 ♗c6; 23. ♕g5 ♖e2+ 24. ♔h1 ♕e6)

126

Chapter 7: The Rosentreter Gambit

Mark Lyell – Peter Varley
Southampton 1986

White to move:

17. ♗g5+ ♔xg5 18. ♘f7+ ♔g6 19. ♘xd8 ♗f6 20. ♕f8 ♘d7 21. ♕g8+ ♗g7 22. ♘e6 1-0

Charles Pigg – Matthew Gross
San Mateo (California) 1992

White to move:

18. ♖xc6+ 1-0

Gellert Papp – Kim Pilgaard
Budapest 2007

White mates in 6:

23. ♗f7+ ♔d8 24. ♖h8 ♕xc2+ 25. ♔xc2 b3+ 26. ♔b1 bxa2+ 27. ♔a1 1-0

Petra Blažková – Martina Valíčková
Havlíčkův Brod 2005

White mates in 6:

19. ♕xc6+ ♗d7 20. ♕xb7 ♖c8 (20... ♕xc2+ 21. ♔xc2 ♗f5+ 22. ♔c1 ♖b8 23. ♕xb8+ ♗c8 24. ♕xc8#) 21. ♕xc8+ 1-0

Chapter 8: Petroff's Defense – Cochrane's Gambit

Markus Wach – Jura Bibik
Münich 1992

White to move:

19. ♕h4 ♘xd5 20. ♕xg4+ ♔h8 21. ♕xh5 ♕b6+ 22. ♔h2 ♘xf4 23. ♕e5+ ♕f6 24. ♕xf6+ ♖xf6 25. g3 ♘h5 26. e5 ♖b6 27. ♖f7 ♖c8 28. b3 ♔g8 29. ♖af1 ♘g7 30. ♖d7 ♘e6 31. ♖ff7 ♘f8 32. ♖xb7 1-0

Stephan Klock – Christoph Klafki
Trier 1992

White mates in 5:

16. ♗h6+ ♔g8 (16...♘xh6 17. ♕xh6+ ♔e8 18. ♘f6#) 17. ♘g5 1-0 (17. ♕e5 ♗f8 18. ♕e8 ♗e6 19. ♕xf8+ ♕xf8 20. ♘f6#)

Dimitri Roman – Jean-Pierre Moulain
Paris 1989

White to move:

17. ♗h6 ♗xh6 18. ♕xh6 ♘f8 (18...♘e7 19. ♕e6+ ♔h8 20. ♘xe7) 19. ♘f6+ ♔h8 20. ♖g5 1-0

Pilar Sogues Tena – Markus Scholz
Rheinland-Pfalz 1990

White to move:

19. ♕xf7 (19...♕xf7 20. e6+) 1-0

Eero Raaste – Asko Hentunen
Finland 1992

White to move:

25. ♖f3 ♕h4 26. ♖f4 ♕g3 (26...♕h6 27. ♕f2 ♔g8 28. ♖f8+) 27. ♖g4 ♕e3+ 28. ♔h2 ♘g7 29. ♕f7 1-0

Chapter 9: The Scotch Gambit

Bjarke Kristensen – Heikki Westerinen
Gausdal 1994

White to move:

20. ♘d4 ♕d7 21. e6 fxe6 22. ♘xe6 ♔f7 23. ♕g5 ♖h7 24. ♘xc5 ♕d8 25. ♘e6 ♕d7 26. ♘xc7 1-0

Ian Rogers – Evgeniy Solozhenkin
Noumea 1995

White to move:

20. ♖h3 ♕e4 (20...♕g4 21. ♘f6+ gxf6 22. ♕h6 ♕g7 23. ♖g3 ♕xg3 24. hxg3 ♔h8 25. ♔f2) 21. ♘f6+ gxf6 22. ♕h6 ♕xf5 23. ♖g3+ ♕g6 24. exf6 ♔h8 25. ♖xg6 ♖g8 26. ♖g7 ♗d3 27. ♖xf7 ♗g6 28. ♖xc7 ♖af8 29. ♖f1 ♖f7 30. ♖xf7 ♗xf7 31. ♖e1 d4 32. ♖e7 ♗g6 33. f7 dxc3 34. fxg8♕+ ♔xg8 35. ♕g7# 1-0

Timothy J. Upton – Andrew D. Martin
Isle of Lewis 1995

Black to move:

20...♖xd4 21. ♖xd4 ♖xd4 22. ♖xd4 (22. ♘xg6 ♖xd1+ 23. ♕f1 f3) ♕b1+ 0-1

Sauli Keskinen – Olli Salmensuu
Helsinki 1998

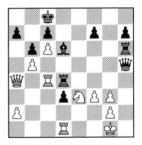

Black mates in three:

28...♕h1+ (Δ 29...♗xg3+) 0-1

Arnaud Fournet – Thierry Gouret
France 2000

Black to move:

11...♘xc3 12. bxc3 ♕xd3 13. ♗xd3 ♗xc3+ 14. ♔e2 ♗xa1 15. ♖xa1 0-0 16.

♖b1 b6 17. ♗b5 ♖ac8 18. h3 ♗f5 19. ♗a4 ♖fd8 20. ♖b2 ♗e4 21. c3 ♘a5 0-1

Giorgi Sulashvili – Matthieu Cornette
Gurzuf 2000

Black mates in four:

15...♘xa2+ 16. ♘xa2 ♕f5 0-1

Vladislav Nevednichy – Zdravko
Vuković, Nikšić 2000

Black to move:

24...♘b4 25. ♗e4 (25. ♗xh7 f6) f5 26. ♗f3 ♘c2+ 27. ♔f1 ♘xa1 28. ♔g2 ♗c6 29. ♗xc6 ♖xd2+ 30. ♔h3 ♖e6 0-1

I. Gontcharova – Tatjana Kostjuk
Orsk 2000

Black to move:

26...♕xd1+ 0-1

Martin Schneider – Sergei Krivoshey
Aschach 2001

Black to move:

15...♖xb2 16. ♕xd8 (16. ♕a4 ♖b4 17. ♕a3 ♖d4+ 18. ♗d2 ♗f4) ♗c2+ (mates) 0-1

Robert Fiala – Petr Císler
Czech Republic 2001

Black to move:

15...♗c5+ 16. ♔e2 (16. ♔e1 ♗b4+ 17. ♕xb4 ♕c1+ 18. ♔f2 ♘xb4 19. ♗b5+ ♔c8 20. a3 ♘c2) ♖e8+ 17. ♔d1 ♗b4 and mates 0-1

Fernando J. M. Costa – Paulo Dias
Portugal 2001

Black mates in two:

30...♗b4+ 0-1

Mehdi Hasan – Hilton Bennett
Kuala Lumpur 2006

Black mates in two:

21...♕xh2+ 0-1

Enrique Garzón – Alexis Ferrara
Buenos Aires 2004

Black to move:

16...♕f5 17. ♔g2 ♗xc5 18. ♗xc5 ♖xd5 19. ♕e2 ♖xc5 20. ♘c3 ♖e8 21. ♕e3 g6 22. ♘e2 ♕xh3+ 23. ♔xh3 ♖h5+ 24. ♔g4 ♘h2+ 0-1

Olivia Smith – Tim Kett
Hensol Park 2006

Black to move:

25...♘e5 26. ♕e2 (26. ♖b3 ♕d6 27. ♖d1 ♖xc4; 26. ♕f2 ♖xd4) ♘d3 27. ♖xb6 ♘xc1 28. ♕e5 ♖xd4 29. ♖xg6 0-1

Herbert Schmid – Volker Scheeff
Bad Homburg 2007

Black to move:

17...♘b4 18. ♖c1 ♘d3+ 0-1

Sergey Daryev – Lyudmila Petrova
Odessa 2007

Black to move:

21...♖d1+ 22. ♔f2 ♖f1+ 23. ♔g3 ♗xf4+ 24. ♔g4 ♗xe3 25. ♗xe3 ♖xa1 0-1

Christopher Briscoe – Ankush Khandelwal, Uxbridge 2009

Black to move:

14...♗xg3 15. fxg3 d3 16. ♗xd3 ♖xd3 17. ♕e2 ♖hd8 18. ♘e4 ♘d419. ♕xd3 ♘xf3+ 20. ♖xf3 ♖xd3 21 . ♖af1 ♕h2# 0-1

Vasiliy Tugarin – Alexander Badmatsyrenov, Irkutsk 2009

Black to move:

18...♖xg5 19. d5 ♗h6 20. ♔h1 ♘b4 21. ♕xe7 ♕d6 22. ♕xd6 cxd6 23. ♘d4 ♖xg2 24. f4 ♖b2 25. ♖f3 ♖gg2 26. h3 ♖gf2 27. ♖e3 ♗xf4 28. ♖e4 ♘d3 29. ♖e7 ♘e5 30. ♖e1 ♗e3 0-1

Piotr Dukaczewski – Martínez Laguna 1996

White to move:

20. ♘xc6 bxc6 (20...♕c7 21. ♘xd8) 21. ♕a6+ ♔b8 22. ♕xc6 ♘d5 23. ♗xd5 ♖xd5 24. ♖xd5 1-0

Gulnara Zhumanbekova – Natalya Grebenschikova, Neftekamsk 2000

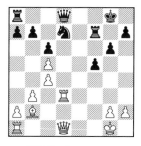

White to move:

21. ♖d6 ♕e7 22. ♕d4 ♘f6 23. ♖xf6 1-0

Javier García Ramos – Vicente Ramón Andrés Julia, Mislata (Spain) 2004

White mates in 5:

18. ♘d6+ cxd6 19. ♕c6+ ♔b8 20. ♗xa6 1-0

Oliver Cooley – Nigel Povah
England 2008

White to move:

16. ♗g5 ♖xd4 17. ♕b3 ♖xd1 18. ♖xd1 ♘d4 19. ♗xh4 fxe4 20. ♖xd4 ♗c5 21. ♕xe6 + ♔b8 22. ♕xe4 1-0

Douglas Sailer – Kris Verhasselt
Leuven 2006

White to move:

18. ♘e5 ♖de7 (on 18...♘xe5, 19. ♕xa7+ mates) 19. g4 1-0 (19...♕xh3 20. ♘xc6+ mates)

Damien André – Guido De Bouver
Belgium 2005

White to move:

23. ♕xb6 ♖xb6 24. ♘f4+ 1-0

Leonardo Duarte – Lucas Liascovich
Villa Martelli 2004

White mates in 5:

19. ♗h6 ♘h5 20. ♖g8+ 1-0

Guy West – Jérôme Lachaux
Queenstown 2006

White to move:

13. ♕e6 ♘b6 (13...♗f7 14. ♕c6+) 14. f5 ♕xd4 15. ♗e3 1-0

Tomás Serra Olives – Antonio Ballester Cladera
Palma de Mallorca 2008

White to move:

18. ♗f4 ♔f8 19. ♖xe7 1-0

Thomas Therkildsen – Wilfried Dehesdin, Le Touquet 2009

White to move:

16. a3 ♕xd1 17. ♖xd1 ♘c2 18. ♖a2 ♘e4 19. f3 ♘d6 20. b3 1-0

Chapter 10: Ruy López – Gajewski Gambit

Viktor Kuznetsov – Grzegorz Gajewski Pardubice 2007

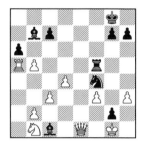

Black to move:

27...♗xf3 28. bxa6 ♘xh3+ 0-1

Manuel Weeks – Stephen Mannion Port Erin 2007

Black to move:

26...♗xe4 0-1 (27. ♗xe4 ♗xf2+ 28. ♔h1 ♘ce3 29. ♗xe3 ♘xe3)

Namig Gouliev – Laurent Fressinet Ajaccio (blitz) 2007

Black to move:

33...Rxf3 34. Nxf3 Rxf3 0-1 (after 35. Qh4, then 35...Rg3+ mates)

Robert Dabo-Peranić – Hrvoje Stević
Bizovac 2008

Black to move:

25...Qf4 0-1 (26. Re5 Bxe5 27. dxe5 Qxg5 28. Qxd5 Rd8)

Amardeep Bartakke – Roy Saptarshi
Mumbai 2008

Black to move:

17...Bf5 0-1 (18. Re2 Bg4)

Dmitry Stets – Axel Delorme
France 2008

White to move:

19. Nd6 1-0 (19...Qe7 20. b4)

Ivan Smikovski – Maxim Lavrov
Novokuznetsk 2008

White to move:

39. Bb4 Rxa7 40. Bxd6 Rd8 41. Bc5 1-0

Oleg Korneev – Jan Willem de Jong
Porto Mannu (Italy) 2008

White to move:

32. Re6 1-0

Pablo Almagro Llanas – Roberto
Pérez García, Burguillos 2008

White to move:

23. ♕c7 1-0 (23...♘c4 24. ♘c6; 23...
♘b7 24. ♖f3 f6 25. ♖g3 g5 26. ♕e7)

Radu Stoenescu – Pierre Amoyal
France 2009

White to move:

23. ♖e5 1-0

Alexander Demianjuk – Alexey
Kondenko, Belorechensk 2009

White to move:

29. ♕d5+ 1-0 (29...♕f7 30. ♗b3)

Chapter 11: The Albin
Countergambit

Aivi Karu – Paul Keres
Corr. 1932

Black mates in four:

25...♖xe4+ 0-1

Edward W. Formanek – D. Oshana
Chicago 1970

Black mates in three:

19...♕xf2+ 20. ♔xf2 ♗c5+ 0-1 (21.
♗e3 ♗xe3#)

Christian Robeson – Antero Harju
Corr. 1990

Black mates in four:

25...♖xf4 0-1 (if 26. exf4 ♕d3#)

♗xg2+ 15. ♔xg2 ♘xf6 0-1

Hans Dinser – Dario Mione
Bratto 1996

Black mates in four:

24...♕xh1+ 0-1

Friedrich Sämisch – Antonio Medina-García, Madrid 1943

Black mates in 5:

18...♘f4+ 19. gxf4 ♖h6 0-1

Hansgeorg Elsas – Wilhelm Ernst
Weidenau 1947

Black to move:

12...♗xf3 13. ♕xf6 ♘e2+ 14. ♔h1

H. Woolverton – O. Pritchard
England 1959

Black to move:

18...♗f3+ 19. ♔h3 (if 19. ♔xf3 ♘d4+) ♖d6 20. ♕d2 g5 (with mate to follow) 0-1

J. Rascher – W. Seemann
Germany 1988

Black to move:

12...♘d3+ 0-1

Elbio Aban – José Bademian
Buenos Aires 1989

Black to move:

19...♘e2+ 0-1 (if 20. ♔h1 ♘xg3+)

José Castillo – José Castro Cajas (Haiti) 1989

Black to move:

13...♖xd4 14. exd4 ♘f3+ (mates) 0-1

Andrés González Garrido – Francisco López Pando, Asturias 1993

Black mates in 5:

18...♘xf3+ 19. exf3 ♗d6+ 0-1

Alexandre Borrás Pardo – Joan Canal Oliveras, Barcelona 1996

Black to move:

12...♘xd4 13. ♕xd7 ♘xf3+ 14. gxf3 ♗xd7 0-1

Jochen Meschke – Dirk Eulberg Hassloch 1997

Black to move:

12...♘e5 13. ♗xb4 ♖xf4 14. h4 ♖f7 0-1

Werner Reyher – Karl-Willi Behle Bad Homburg 2000

Black to move:

17...♘f5 0-1

J. Choque – Jesus García Pío Lima 2000

Black to move:

14...d3 15. ♖e1 (15. f3 dxe2 16. ♕xe2 ♘xf3+ 17. ♗xf3 ♕xe2) 15...dxe2 16. ♖xe2 (16. ♕c2 ♘d3) ♕f6 17. ♖b1 ♘xc4 18. ♕a4 ♘xd2 19. ♕xa7 ♕a6 20. ♕c5 0-1

Markus Bachmann – Hans J. Thomi
Scuol 2001

Black to move:

11...♗d4 12. ♘xd4 ♘xd4 13. ♔f2 ♘b3 14. ♖a2 ♘xc1 0-1

Nadhmia Othman – Elisabeth
Shaughnessy, Bled 2002

Black to move:

15...♘d4 16. ♕d3 (16. ♕a4+ b5 17. ♘xe3) ♕xf2+ 17. ♔d1 ♕xg2 18. ♖e1 ♕f3+ 19. ♖e2 ♕f1+ 20. ♖e1 ♕xd3# 0-1

Ekaterina Rybakova – Nikolay
Dubiaga, Krasnodar 2006

Black to move:

20...♕g5 0-1

Mukhit Ismailov – Viktoria Bukhteeva
Tomsk 2008

Black to move:

16...♕xb2 17. ♖a2 0-1 (17...♕xa2)

Erich Gigerl – Federico Cirabisi
Caorle 1988

Black to move:

18...♖xh4 19. gxh4 ♘f3+ 20. ♘xf3 gxf3 21. ♕d2 ♘e4 0-1

Pavel Košnář – Vratislav Kohout
Czech Republic 1996

Black to move:

21...Rxf2+ 0-1(22. Rxf2 ♘e3+)

Henk-Jan Paalman – Jochem
Snuverink, Deventer 1998

Black to move:

17...♘d3+ 18. ♔f1 ♕h4 19. exd3
♗xd3+ 20. ♔e1 ♕xh1+ 21. ♘f1 ♕xf1+
22. ♔d2 ♕xa1 23. b6 ♕b2+ 24. ♔xd3
♕xa3+ 0-1

Víctor García Brodersen – Boerries
Grabenhorst, Kassel 2000

Black to move:

15...♕f2+ 16. ♔d1 Rad8+ 17. ♗d2
♘e3+ 18. ♔c1 ♘xf1 19. g4 ♘g3 20. ♕b3
♘xh1 21. gxf5 ♕xe2 22. ♕c3 Rd3 0-1

Fernando Braga – Andrés Pons
Aguilera, Binissalem 2003

Black mates in 7:

18...♗f3+ 19. gxf3 gxf3+ 20. ♔xf3
♕h3+ 21. ♔e4 Rh4+ 22. f4 ♕g2+ 0-1

Martin Wilde – Hans-Joachim Vatter
Germany 1989

White mates in three:

18. ♕xa7+ 1-0

Antonio P. Santos – Nuno Rodrigues
Almada 1998

White mates in four:

17. ♕a8+ ♔d7 18. ♕xd8+ 1-0

Denis Goltsov – K. Patsyuk
Kaluga 2003

White to move:

16. ♗xe5 fxe5 (16...♖xd1+ 17. ♖xd1)
17. ♗h3+ 1-0

Dirk Hummel – Titus Ensinks
Groningen 2001

White to move:

15. ♗xb7+ ♔b8 16. ♘xd7+ ♗xd7 17.
♕a2 ♘xb7 18. b4 1-0

Peter Östberg – Matts Unander
Sundsvall 1979

White to move:

13. ♘e5 ♘xe5 (13...♗xg2 14. ♘xd7
♗xf1 15. ♘e5 ♗xd2 16. ♘xc6) 14. ♗xb7+
♔xb7 15. ♕xb4+ ♔c6 16. ♗a3 ♘f3+ 17.
♘xf3 1-0

Jens Hartung-Nielsen – Jorgen
Hvenekilde, Copenhagen 1980

White to move:

14. f5 f6 (14...♘e5 15. f6 gxf6
16. ♘xf6#) 15. fxg6 fxg5 16.
♘xg5 hxg6 17. ♕f3 ♖b8 18. ♕f7+
♔d8 19. ♘e6+ ♔c8 20. ♘xf8 1-0

David R. MacDonald – Richard D.
Westwood, London 1980

White to move:

11. ♘xc6 bxc6 12. ♕a4 ♔b7 (12...a5
13. ♕xa5 ♔b8 14. ♘a3 ♖c8 15. ♘b5) 13.
♕b5+ 1-0

141

Matthias Rech – H. Betz
Ladenburg 1992

White to move:

14. ♗xb7+ 1-0 (14...♔xb7 15. ♘c5+)

Petr Čekan – Jakub Čmiko
Klatovy 2005

White to move:

10. ♗xc6+ bxc6 11. ♕h5+ g6 12.
♕xc5 ♘f6 13. ♕xc6+ ♔f7 14. exd4 1-0

János Mizsei – Frank Grube
Budapest 2006

White to move:

10. ♘xe5 1-0 (10...♘xe5 11. ♕a4+)

Chapter 12: The Winawer Countergambit

Florian Handke – Arcadio Cieza
Stuttgart 1998

White mates in three:

21. ♘xg7+ ♔f8 22. ♖d8+ 1-0

Mikhail Gurevich – Jeroen Piket
Antwerp 1993

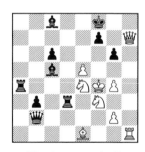

Black mates in 5:

31...♖xe4+ 32. ♔xe4 ♖d4+ 33. ♔e3
♖xg4+ 34. ♘d4 ♗xd4+ 35. ♔d3 ♕c2#
0-1

Hubert van Kooten – Jildo Kalma
Haarlem 2000

Black to move:

23...♘xe6 24. ♘xe6 ♗c4 25. ♘xc5 ♗xb3 26. ♘xb3 ♕d5+ 27. ♔h3 ♖xe2 28. ♖hd1 ♕f5+ 0-1

Murtas Kazhgaleyev – Bjarke Sahl
Port Erin 2006

White to move:

21. ♗xd5+ cxd5 22. ♕b3 1-0

Ivan Filippov – Viacheslav Rozkov
Orsk 2002

Black to move:

29...♗b3 30. ♖e1 ♘d5 (30...♗d5 31. ♖a6 ♕c4 32. b4 ♕b3+ 33. ♕b2 ♕d3+

34. ♔a1 ♖c2) 31. ♘e4 ♗c2+ 0-1

Michal Krasenkow – Predrag Nikolić
Bled 2002

Black to move:

17...♗xc3 18. ♕xc3 ♘f2 0-1

Alexander Beliavsky – Boris Gelfand
Linares 1992

White to move:

22. ♗e6+ ♔h8 23. ♖xf6 ♘d7 24. ♖xg6 1-0

Attila Vass – Thilo Keskowski
Eger 1992

White to move:

13. ♗g5 e3 14. ♗xe7 ♗e4 15. f3 ♖xd4 16. cxd4 ♗xf3 1-0

Dragan Barlov – Ville Lehto
Helsinki 1990

White to move:

23. ♘cd5 ♗xd5 (23...♕a7 24. ♗b4+ ♔f7 25. ♘e7 ♖c7 26. ♕c4+) 24. ♕xc8+ ♔f7 25. ♕d7+ ♔g6 26. ♗c1 ♗e6 27. ♕xd4 1-0

Jan Timman – Jonny Hector
Malme 2007

Black to move:

22...♕f5 23. ♕c3 ♘ge3+ 24. ♔g1 ♘xg2 25. ♔xg2 ♖xe2 26. ♘f4 ♕e4+ 27. ♕f3 ♕xf3+ 28. ♔xf3 ♖e1 0-1

Nicolas Gérard – Bruno Steiner
Budapest 2003

White to move:

29. ♗xf6 ♘xe1 30. ♗e5 ♘xf3 31. ♕e8+ ♕d8 (31...♕c8 32. ♗xd6+) 32. ♗xd6+ (32. ♕xd8#) ♔c8 1-0

Eiitsa Raeva – Monika Dilova
Pernik 2004

White to move:

29. ♖f5 ♘e5 30. ♕h3 ♔c7 31. dxe5 ♕xa2 32. e6 ♖b1 33. ♖xf7+ ♔c6 34. ♕f3+ ♔c5 35. ♕f5+ 1-0

Ralf Åkesson – Chiel van Oosterom
Wijk aan Zee 2007

White to move:

24. ♖xe7 ♖xe7 25. ♗xf6 gxf6 (25... ♖f7 26. ♗e7+ mates) 26. ♕g8# 1-0

144

Chapter 13: The Geller Gambit

Giovanni Vallifuoco – Umberto Sodano, Naples 1989

White to move:

14. ♘xf7 ♕d7 (14...♔xf7 15. ♕h5+) 15. ♘d6+ ♕xd6 16. ♕h5+ ♗f7 17. ♕xb5+ ♘d7 18. ♗xa8 ♕e6+ 19. ♗e3 ♕b6 20. ♗c6 ♗e6 21. 0-0 1-0

Martin J. Cutmore – Mary Jones England 2001

White to move:

13. ♖xa6 ♗xa6 (13...♗b4 14. ♖xe6+) 14. ♕f3 ♕d5 (14...f5 15. ♕c6+) 15. ♕xf7+♔d8 16. ♘xe6+ ♕xe6 17. ♕xe6 ♗c8 18. ♕f6+ 1-0

Eduard Porper – Kieran O'Driscoll Guernsey 2006

White to move:

14. ♗a3 1-0

John Fedorowicz – Martin Klebel Bad Mergentheim 1988

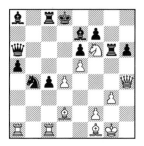

White to move:

27. ♗xb4 ♗xb4 28. ♘d5+ ♔e8 29. ♘xb4 ♕b7 30. ♘c2 1-0

Volker Schmidt – H. Giesen Menden 1974

White mates in 6:

27. ♗c5+ ♕xc5 28. ♕g5+ 1-0

Svetomir Randjelović – Sasko Ristevski, Zürich 1999

White to move:

20. ♕f3 ♘d5 21. ♘f6+ 1-0

Vincent McCambridge – Edward Formanek, Lone Pine 1979

White to move:

13. ♗f4 ♔f7 (13...♘xa1 14. ♘c7+ ♔f7 15. ♘xa8 ♘c2 16. ♘e5+ ♔g8 17. ♕xc2) 14. ♘e5+ ♔e8 15. ♗xe6 ♗xe6 16. ♕xc2 axb5 17. ♖xa8 ♗d5 18. ♖a7 ♗xg2 19. ♖c1 1-0

M. Przybyl – Janusz Kwiek Corr. 1994

White to move:

26. ♗b3 ♕d3+ 27. ♔g1 1-0

Garry Kasparov – computer Rotterdam 1987

White to move:

15. ♗xh6 gxh6 (15...♗xc3 16. ♗g5 f6 17. bxc3) 16. ♘xd5 exd5 17. ♘f6+ ♔g7 18. f4 ♕b7 19. ♖f3 ♕c6 20. f5 ♖h8 21. ♖af1 ♗d2 22. e6 ♖f8 23. ♘g4 ♕b6 24. f6+ ♔h7 25. e7 ♕xd4+ 26. ♔h1 ♘c6 27. ♖h3 ♕xb2 28. ♘xh6 1-0

Dušan Rajković – Lothar Olzem Bad Mergentheim 1988

White to move:

22. ♗xd5 ♕xd5 23. ♘e4 1-0 (23...0-0-0 24. ♖d2 ♘d4 25. ♗xd4)

Loek van Wely – Paulus A. Boersma
Enschede 1990

White to move:

22. ♗h5+ ♘g6 (if 22...g6, then 23. ♘f6+ ♔d8 24. ♖d1+ mates) 23. ♘g5 1-0 (23...♖f8 24. ♘xh7)

Carmen Feil – Swantje Strassmann
Germany 1991

White to move:

15. dxe6 fxe6 (15...♗xb5 16. exf7+ ♔xf7 17. ♕b3+ ♔e8 18. axb5) 16. ♘e5 1-0 (on 16...♗xb5, 17. ♕h5+ leads to mate)

Carolyn Withgitt – Robert Whitaker
USA 1994

White to move:

23. ♖xf6 ♔xf6 24. dxc5 ♔e7 25. c6 ♖fc8 26. ♖xb7+ 1-0

S. Alberto García – Sergio Medina
Los Barrios (Spain) 1995

White to move:

12. ♕e4 (12...♗xf3 13. ♗xf3) 1-0

Oleg Burlai – Vitaly Melnic
Alushta 1999

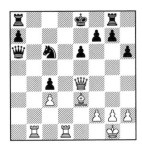

White to move:

24. ♖d6 ♖c8 25. ♖xe6+ ♔d7 (25... fxe6 26. ♕xe6+ ♔f8 27. ♗c5+) 26. ♕d5+ 1-0

Michael Jorgensen – Sandra De
Blecourt, Copenhagen 2001

White to move:

18. ♗xf5 exf5 19. ♘e6 ♕c8 20. ♘xg7+ ♔f8 (20...♔d8 21. ♘f7+) 21. ♕h5 (checkmating) 1-0

Sebastien Cossin – Anthony Denisart
Rosny-sous-Bois 2002

White to move:

19. ♘d6+ ♗xd6 (19...♔d7 20. ♗xd5 ♗xd6 21. exd6 ♔xd6 22. ♖xe6+) 20. ♗xd5 ♘b4 (20...exd5 21. exd6+ ♘e7; 20...♕b6 21. exd6) 21. cxb4 1-0

Rudolf Meessen – Gerard Welling
Belgium 2003

White to move:

18. ♘e4 cxb5 (18...♗c8 19. ♘d6 ♕h7 20. ♘xc8 ♖xc8 21. b6) 19. ♘d6 ♗xg2 20. ♘xf5 ♗xf1 21. ♘e7+ ♔h8 22. ♖xf1 a5 23. f4 c3 24. f5 exf5 25. ♘xf5 ♖a6 26. d5 b4 27. d6 c2 28. ♘xh6 gxh6 29. ♕xh6+ ♔g8 30. ♖f5 1-0

Bernd Kievelitz – Colin S. Crouch
Děčín 1996

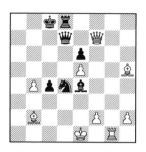

Black mates in four:

23...♘c2+ 24. ♔f1 ♕d3+ 0-1

Merlijn Silvester Donk – Dimitri
Komarov, Leeuwarden 1995

Black to move:

22...♗h5+ 23. g4 ♕h4 24. gxh5 ♕h3+ 25. ♔e4 ♘d7 26. ♖xf8+ ♔xf8 27. ♗xe6 ♘f6+ 0-1

Fritz Maurer – Philip Müller
Zürich 1990

Black to move:

15...♘xd4 16. cxd4 (16. ♔d1 ♘e2+, mating) ♕xd4 17. ♕xd8+ (17. f3 ♗b4+) ♔xd8 18. ♗g5+ ♔c8 19. ♖d1 ♗b4+ 20. ♔e2 ♕e4+ 0-1

Martti Tepponen – Pentti Hietanen
Corr. 1962

Black to move:

17...♕e4+ (Δ 18...♕b1+) 0-1

Frank Hegermann – Ralf Widera
Mainz 1996

Black to move:

17...♘xd4 18. cxd4 ♗b4+ 19. ♔e2
♕xd4 20. ♕xd8+ ♕xd8 0-1

László Vadász – Iulia Mashinskaya
Budapest 1997

Black to move:

28...♘c3 29. ♕h5 (29. ♗f4 ♖e2 30.
♖xe2 ♘xe2+ 31. ♔h2 b2) ♖xc1 30. ♖xc1
b2 0-1

Chapter 14: The Blumenfeld Gambit

Andreas Schmied – Rasmus Svane
Helsingor 2008

Black to move:

13...♗f6 14. a3 ♘a6 15. f4 d6 16. e4
dxe5 17. ♗b5+ ♔f8 18. 0-0 exf4 19. ♗c4
♘c7 20. ♖xf4 ♗e6 0-1

Luis César Martín – Jonathan Alonso
Moyano, Tenerife 2003

Black to move:

19...♖xd5 0-1 (20. ♖xd5 ♕c6)

Jovanović – Raimundo García
Santa Fe (Argentina) 1973

Black to move:

20...Rxe1+ 21. Nxe1 Qe5 0-1

Tony Miles – Lev Alburt
Philadelphia 1989

Black to move:

21...d4 22. exd4 Bf3 23. Ne4 Bxe4
24. Rxe4 Rf2 25. Qe8+ Nf8 0-1

Néstor Daniel Robledo – Lucas Moreda
Tres Arroyos (Argentina) 1994

Black to move:

14...c2 15. Qc1 Qc3+ 0-1

Sylwia Gapa – Monika Krupa
Warsaw 2004

Black to move:

23...Qc3+ 24. Nd2 Bxd2+ 0-1

Guillaume Camus de Solliers –
Christopher Debray, Pau 2008

Black to move:

24...Ne6 25. Qf2 Nxf4 0-1

Heimo Loebler – Adolivio Capece
Caorle 1989

Black to move:

18...Bb4 19. Bxf6 (19. Qb2
Rxd4 20. Qxd4 Bc5) Rxf6 20.
Qc1 Bd2 21. Qb2 Bxf4 22. g3
Be5 23.Qc1 Rxf1+ 24.Bxf1 Bxa1
25.Qxa1 Qc5+ 26.Nf2 Rd2 0-1

Alexey Shaliapin – Sergey A. Ivanov
Petrozavodsk 2007

Black to move:

SOLUTIONS

14...♕e5 15. f4 exf3 0-1

Rob Bodicker – Deep Sengupta
Vlissingen 2007

Black to move:

21...c3 22. ♘xe5 (22. ♖c1 ♘xc1 23. ♗xc1 ♗d6) c2 23. ♖c1 cxd1♕ 24. ♖xc7 ♕xd2 0-1

Michael Kuraszkiewicz – Radosław
Wojtaszek, Warsaw 2007

Black to move:

30...♗xe3 0-1

Stavros Maliaros – Sotiris Karafidis
Greece 1983

White to move:

21. ♕xg6 ♗f4 (better is 21...♗xd5 22. ♕xd6 ♘d7 23. ♕xf8+) 22. ♖d8 1-0

Eugenio Szabados – Gisela Kahn
Gresser, Venice 1970

White to move:

22. ♘d7 ♖fd8 23. ♘f6+ ♔g7 24. ♘xd5 ♖xd5 25. ♗e4 1-0

Zurab Azmaiparashvili – Evgenij
Miroshnichenko, Kallithea 2009

White mates in 5:

19. ♘a7+ 1-0 (if 19...♖xa7, then 20. ♕e8+ ♔c7 21. ♕d8+ followed by 22. ♖d6+)

Podzerov – Kuntzević
Corr. 1971

White to move:

18. ♕h5 ♘d7 (18...♖f8 19. ♘f7+
♔h8 20. ♘5g7+) 19. ♕xf7+ ♔h8 20.
♕g8+ (mates) 1-0

Fernando Sanz Bastos – Andrés
Reglero, Asturias 1985

White to move:

18. ♘h6+ 1-0

Thomas Rosenhöfer – Weil
East Germany 1989

White to move:

20. ♗e4 ♖b8 21. ♗d5 ♖xe5 22. ♘xe5
♘xe5 23. ♖xe5 ♕h4 24. ♗xf7+ 1-0

Chapter 15: Queen's Indian
Defense – Polugaevsky Variation

Marcelo Tempone – Armando López
Jiménez, Córdoba 1980

White mates in 3:

18. ♘xf7+ 1-0 (18...gxh5 19. ♗e4+
♔g8 20. ♘h6#)

Garry Kasparov – Slavoljub
Marjanović, Malta 1980

White to move:

20. ♘xh7 ♕d4 21. ♕h5 g6 22. ♕h4
♗xa1 23. ♘f6+ 1-0

Hans Strobel – Kai Schönwolff
Hamburg 1989

White to move:

21. Rxd6 Rxd6 22. Re7 Rd7 23. Rxd7 1-0

Zoran Veličković – Oliver Riemelmoser
Graz 1994

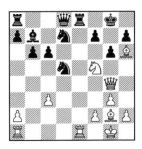

White to move:

18. Rxe8+ Wxe8 19. Bxd5 cxd5 20. Nd6 Ne5 21. We2 We7 22. Nxb7 Re8 23. f4 Nc4 24. Wxe7 Rxe7 25. Nd8 Na5 26. Bg5 Rd7 27. Re1 Kg7 28. Re8 Rc7 29. Re7 Rxc3 30. Ne6+ 1-0

Vojtěch Pliva – Michal Tocháček
Prague 1995

White to move:

15. b4 Na4 (15...Ncxe4 16. Nxe7+ Wxe7 17. Wd4 d5 18. f3; 15...Ne6 16. Nd5; 15...Nb7 16. b5) 16. Nxe7+ Wxe7 17. Nxa4 Wb7 18. Nc3 Rfe8 19. Bg5 Re5 20. Bxf6 gxf6 21. f4 Ree8 22. b5 Bd7 23. e5 Wc7 24. Nd5 Wc5+ 25. Kh1 1-0

Karl-Heinz Podzielny – Udo Düssel
Schwäbisch Gmünd 1998

White to move:

21. Rxe6 Wc7 (21...fxe6 22. Wxe6+ Kg7 23. Nf5+) 22. Re2 1-0

Josef Vařejčko – Josef Sýkora
Czech Republic 2001

White to move:

19. Ne4 d5 (19...Bb4 20. Wg4) 20. Wg4 1-0

153

Sergei Krivoshey – Hans Gerl
Schwäbisch Gmünd 2002

White to move:

19. ♗e5 ♕g6 20. ♕xg6 hxg6 21. ♘d6
♘d8 22. ♘xc8 ♗xc8 23. ♗xb8 1-0

Shakhriyar Mamedyarov – Dmitry
Jakovenko, Fügen 2006

White to move:

23. ♗d5 1-0 (23...♗xd5 24. ♕xd5+
♔h8 25. ♘f7+)

Miloš Pavlović – Ivan Žaja
Županja 2007

White to move:

20. ♕xe2 ♖xe2 21. ♗c8 a5 22. ♖e1

♖e6 23. ♗xe6 fxe6 24. ♗e5 ♔f7 25.
♖ad1 ♔e7 26. ♗d6+ ♔f7 27. ♗c7 b5 28.
♖d6 ♗xb2 29. ♖d8 c5 30. ♖b1 1-0

Bandyopadhyay Roktim – Roi
Miedema, Dieren 2006

White to move:

28. ♖xe5 1-0 (28...♕xe5 29. ♕b3+)

Anatoliy Polivanov – Konstantin
Borsuk, Lvov 2005

White to move:

29. ♕xh3 ♖xh3 30. ♗g2 1-0 (30...
♖h8 31. ♖e7+)

János Szabolcsi – Markku Henttinen
Budapest 1981

White to move:

23. ♗c6 h5 24. ♕d1 ♘xf4 25. ♗xd7 ♖xd7 26. gxf4 ♘c5 27. ♕xh5 ♖e8 28. ♖d1 ♖e6 29. ♘g3 ♖de7 30. ♔g2 g6 31. ♕g4 1-0

Sorin Opincă – Victor Ianocichin
Kishinev 2008

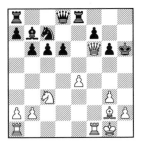

White to move:

22. ♕xd8 ♖exd8 23. ♖xf7 ♖ac8 24. ♗h3 d5 25. ♗xc8 ♖xc8 26. exd5 cxd5 27. ♖c1 d4 28. ♘e2 d3 29. ♖cxc7 dxe2 30. ♔f2 ♖e8 31. ♖ce7 ♖xe7 32. ♖xe7 ♗d5 33. ♖xa7 1-0

Frode Urkedal – Nicolai Getz
Oslo 2009

White to move:

23. ♗e4 ♘xe1 (23...♘xe5 24. ♗h7+ ♔h8 25. ♗d3+) 24. ♗h7+ ♔h8 25. ♗c2+ ♔g8 26. ♗b3+ ♖f7 27. exf6 ♕xf6 28. ♗xf7+ ♔f8 29. ♕b4+ ♕e7 30. ♕xe7+ ♔xe7 31. ♗d2 1-0

Piotr Hoszowski – A. Stechnij
Corr. 1993

Black to move:

24...♖xd1 25. ♖xd1 ♗f1 26. ♕d6 ♗xg2+ 27. ♔g1 ♗xe4 0-1

Notes